Wallace-Homestead
Price Guide to
BASKETS

Wallace-Homestead
Price Guide to
BASKETS
Second Edition

Frances Johnson

Wallace-Homestead Book Company
Radnor, Pennsylvania

Cover and text design: Anthony Jacobson

Library of Congress Cataloging in Publication

Thompson-Johnson, Frances, 1920–
    Wallace-Homestead price guide to baskets / Frances Johnson.—2nd ed.
       p.   cm.
    Previous 1987 ed. by Frances Thompson-Johnson.
    ISBN 0-87069-542-8
    1. Basketwork—United States—Collectors and collecting—Catalogs.
I. Thompson-Johnson, Frances, 1920– Wallace-Homestead price guide to baskets. II. Title.   III. Title: Price guide to baskets.
NK3649.5.T47   1989   89-16635
746.41′2′075—dc20   CIP

2 3 4 5 6 7 8 9 0   8 7 6 5 4 3 2 1

To
Kim Johnson

Contents

Acknowledgments

It is impossible to thank all the people who help an author assemble material for a book, but there are always those special few who are so helpful that they deserve more than a simple verbal thank you. Deserving of special thanks are Elsie Kilmer, Knightstown, Indiana; Peggy Merritt, Falmouth, Maine; Louis Black, Oxford Mall, Oxford, Maine; Jim and Rose Cyr, Cyr Auctions, Bryant Pond, Maine; Amity Furniture Strippers, Westbrook, Maine; Faye Stouff, Jeanerette, Louisiana; The Peter Smith Terry Basket Collection, Dr. Chris Marshall, and Unity College, Unity, Maine; Phill McIntyre and Daughters, Auctions, and Barlow's Antiques, Anson, Maine; Miccosukee Indian Village, Miami, Florida; Regina Hines, Ball Ground, Georgia; Caroline French and Parker-French Antique Center, Northwood, New Hampshire; Anne Chester, Window Rock, Arizona; Dr. Ann Bailey, Tucson, Arizona; Basketville, Putney, Vermont; Lightner Museum, St. Augustine, Florida; Thomas J. Sabiston, U.S. Army Aviation Museum, Ft. Rucker, Alabama; Blount Mansion, Knoxville, Tennessee; Pike Museum, Troy, Alabama; Chief To-Me-Kin, Wells, Maine; Doug Fernald, Penobscot Indian Museum, Rosalie Clark, and Eunice Crawley, Indian Island, Old Town, Maine; Stephen Zeh, Temple, Maine; Ron and Anne Riendeau Auctions, Topsham, Maine; Mary Vanderhorst, Mt. Pleasant, South Carolina; Maritime Museum, Bath, Maine; and Bonnie Aaskov, Cider Mill Antique Mall, Windham, Maine.

Wallace-Homestead
Price Guide to
BASKETS

Introduction

There is a tendency to call any container that has a handle a *basket,* and any container without a handle a *box*. However, the dictionary describes a basket as "a container made of interwoven materials such as rushes, twigs, and strips of wood." No mention is made of a handle—just of a container.

Our ancestors made some very interesting containers of interwoven rushes, twigs, strips of wood, and grasses, and by accepting the "container theory," we basket collectors find that a whole new world of collecting is opened up to us. We do not need to let an absence of handles stand in our way.

The use of woven or basketry items goes back to ancient times. Early civilizations used woven basketry items for all their needs; there were no other containers at the time. Indians used basketry to make everything from canoes to containers for food and water, long before the European settlers arrived.

The Pilgrims

We know that basketry was an accepted craft for the Pilgrims and had been for a long time before they even set sail for the New World. Basketmaking was well enough established to warrant a basketmakers guild in England as early as 1569. The guild was designed to protect the users of baskets— as a sort of weight and measurement inspection. Since goods were often purchased by the peck or bushel, and the only means of measurement were the baskets, it was important for a basket to hold a full measure. Thus, the guild was organized and commissioned to check baskets in the same way the scale at the fruit market is checked

for accuracy. If a basket was found to be undersize, it was confiscated and burned.

The Pilgrims brought this feeling of fair play with them to the New World. Once here, they exchanged basketmaking ideas with the Indians. By combining methods, both the Indians and Pilgrims probably ended up using the best and easiest methods.

Old records show how important baskets were in the lives of the early settlers and how much baskets were treasured. In fact, the settlers valued baskets enough to mention them in their wills and inventories. Several inventories of the 1600s list winnowing baskets, as well as bushel and half-bushel baskets.

Early Settlers

The early settlers, as well as some of the later ones, used basketry to make necessities, as well as to create a few luxuries. They made weirs, fish and eel traps for trapping food, and cradles for their newborn babies. They made baskets to be used for planting, gathering, and storing. They made picnic baskets, doll cradles, fans, napkin rings, and jewelry baskets. All of these items were coiled or woven out of the materials available to each individual basketmaker.

Necessity is the mother of invention, they say. Since the settlers didn't have paper bags or boxes, nor did they have plastic containers as we do now, it was essential for them to make some kind of container. Baskets were easily and cheaply made, as the fields and forests were full of materials.

Americans have never lost their love of basketry. Maybe using baskets is a habit, and Americans became so accustomed to using them that it was only natural that they continue to do so. Whatever the reason, that is exactly what they did. They continued to make and use baskets long after other containers became available. Not as many as before, perhaps, but still they continued with their basketry, and now they had more time to experiment with fancy baskets, miniatures, and novelties. Incidentally, *basketry* is defined as the craft or process of making baskets; the term may also be used to describe baskets collectively.

Americans later began to use basketry techniques to make furniture—wicker furniture. Originally, this furniture was called "basket furniture"; only in recent years has the name been changed to *wicker*.

The Rebirth of Basketry

Through the years, the popularity of baskets has experienced many highs and lows. Perhaps the biggest lull in basketmaking came right after World War II, when new inventions and materials began flooding the market. The country was slowly changing and there was little or no demand for baskets, not even old ones.

This changed drastically, however, a decade or so ago, when basketmaking and collecting reached a new high. Never before had there been so many people making, selling, and teaching basketry. As it has always been, the fascination for basketmaking appeals to both men and women; yet recently, there has been a surprising amount of interest in basketmaking by business executives who have learned to make baskets for its relaxation value. Others have gone into it as a profession, making baskets to sell to a basket-loving public.

Classes in basketry are very popular both at local colleges and on Indian reservations. Current prices for baskets, both old and new, have encouraged many young women to enroll in basketry classes. These new basketmakers enjoy the satisfaction of creating baskets; also, it's inexpensive, and the actual basketmaking process is both rewarding and relaxing.

For the past several years it has been rare to find a magazine that doesn't include pictures that show baskets in them—usually as room decorations. And it's refreshing to find frequent articles in local newspapers describing the accomplishments of local individuals involved in basketmaking. Basketmaking has never had so many devotees.

Using This Book

Almost all natural-material baskets are handmade, which means that each one will be at least somewhat different from all others. Thus, it's practically impossible to find two that are identical in every way. The size of baskets can be extremely misleading in photographs; for instance, a closeup lens can make the smallest basket look like a large cotton basket. For that reason, this book includes measurements for each basket pictured (most measurements are to the nearest $\frac{1}{4}$ inch). In addition, the picture captions use letters to provide measurement descriptions, as follows:

h	height
o.h.	overall height, including handle
l	length
w	width
dia	diameter at the widest point
sq	square

About Prices

Trying to pin down an exact price on anything, new items as well as antiques, can be difficult. The same item may be priced differently from one store to another in a certain area, but when comparing the prices in one location to those in another, the differences can be mind-boggling. This is especially true for baskets.

I encountered a glaring example of how different prices can be within the same area early in 1989 when I attended an auction in a nearby town. A lovely, miniature oak-splint basket sold for $275. A week later, in the same town, I attended an antique show, where a similar, if not identical, basket was priced at $600. We expect prices to vary from one location to another, but this was in the same town! An investigation into the prices on scale baskets turned up the same kind of variance. On a one-day, 50- to 60-mile trip to area malls, I found six similar scale baskets priced from $8 to $60 each.

Baskets always bring higher prices in the areas where they are made and where the collectors are familiar with them. For instance, the pine needle baskets made in the South are not nearly as sought after in the North, nor will they bring prices in the North that are equivalent to the prices they bring in the South. Another example is the Gullah baskets made in South Carolina. Outside the South they are barely known, and prices are very low. Baskets made by the Indians in the Southwest bring much higher prices in that area than they do in the Northeast. By the same token, the ash-splint baskets and souvenir items made for the turn-of-the-century tourist trade are not very well known in areas outside the Northeast, nor do they bring the same prices as in the Northeast. Another specific example is a New Hampshire basket in excellent condition that sold recently at auction for $550. A similar basket in good condition was priced at $150 in a shop in a different area.

The previous examples should help to explain the wide price ranges given in this book. The lower price in a range might represent what New Englanders are willing to pay for pine needle baskets, for example, while the higher price might be the going price for the same baskets in the South.

Prices in this book are intended to be used strictly as *guides,* and they are based on prices seen on baskets all around the country. In an effort to get as much up-to-date information on baskets as possible, we took a trip through New England recently. The most noticeable thing we found was a lack of good baskets. Most were damaged in some way; some badly, others only slightly. Prices were higher than we had seen six months earlier on a similar trip, and the baskets were not the same quality as they had been then. There was also a noticeable increase in rattan basketry items from 30 to 50 years ago. Half a decade or so ago you could hardly have given them away; now they start in the $15-to-$20 bracket. There was also an increase in the number of Oriental baskets being offered. They, too, were priced higher than they had been in recent years, in some cases as much as 100 percent higher. A pretty, Oriental, two-tiered pie basket with brass fittings and a lock, badly damaged, was "sale priced" at $75.

River- and swamp-cane baskets, especially those half a century old or older, are bringing the best prices in the South (with the exception of swing handle baskets, which are the best sellers and the most expensive in all areas of the country). Old Indian coiled baskets are more popular and expensive in the Southwest.

The best advice anyone can give to beginning basket collectors is to study the types of baskets they like best, and then do a lot of price comparisons. You should never buy a basket that you feel is overpriced until you have shopped in many places. Unless it is a basket you have been searching for for a long time, or one so rare you doubt you'll ever see another, take a little time to investigate and think it over before making the purchase.

Basketry from A to Z

Abenaki Indians

Although the Abenaki Indians lived on the reservation on the St. Francis River in Quebec, they spent their summers from 1870 through 1920 in the resort towns of Old Forge, Saratoga Lake, Lake Mahopak, and Lake George, New York; Ottawa Beach, Michigan; Asbury Park and Atlantic City, New Jersey; and the White Mountains of New Hampshire. They went to the resort towns to make and sell baskets.

In the winter they worked at home making baskets to sell at the resorts during the summer. According to reports, some of the more popular makers couldn't keep up with the demand, and therefore hired others who only wanted to work summers. The Abenakis rented houses and shops in and near the resort areas where they established their basket businesses.

Meanwhile, other Abenaki basketmakers, who preferred to stay home on the reservation in the summer, worked for the large wholesalers who found such a demand

Covered basket, ash splint, souvenir type, Unity College collection. $38–$75

for the baskets that they mailed out catalogs. Many of the basketmakers who worked the resort areas reported making between $4000 and $5000 a year, not a measly amount for those times.

The basketmakers living in New England might not have been as involved as the

Wall-hanging basket, type made by the Abenakis. 4½" w, 11" l, 9" h. $45–$89

Fancy ash-splint basket. 4" dia, 4½" h. $40–$65

Another style of souvenir basket, ash splint, Unity College collection. $48–$70

Abenakis, but they were in the middle of the tourist areas and could stay home with their roadside stands and do contract work for the Shakers as well. When the basket production all over the country is combined for this period, it's easy to see why there are still so many baskets and basketry items available to the collector.

Acorn-Picking Baskets

Customs varied with each tribe of Indian, and of course their locations influenced customs to a degree. But regardless of location or custom, there was only one acorn harvest per year; therefore, the acorns had to be

Depending on location and tribe, this elm basket may have been used for gathering. 20" l, 9" w, 14" o.h. Slightly damaged, $125–$160.

Cherokees may have used this basket for storing acorns or meal. River-cane covered basket. $600–$900

gathered and stored as quickly as possible. The men and boys climbed the trees and shook them to make acorns fall so the women and children could pick them up. Some tribes designed their own acorn scoops, or nut scoops, so the acorns could be picked up with as little effort as possible; others continued to crawl around on the ground, picking up the nuts a few at a time.

Once the acorns were gathered, it was the women's chore to transform the bitter acorn into tasty food—a chore in which they were well skilled. Nevertheless, it was a long and tiring one. First, the acorns had to be shelled. This required cracking the shells gently, and then picking out the kernels. Two baskets were required for this job: the picking-and-storing basket and another for the shelled kernels. Then, using a crude apparatus resembling a mortar and pestle, the women ground the acorns into meal. To remove the tannin that not only made a very bitter taste but was considered dangerous to one's health if too much was consumed, they would dig a hole in the sand, pack acorn meal around the sides, and then pour hot water over the meal until most of the tannin was gone. Finally, the acorn meal was ready to be made into bread or soup.

Acorn Scoop

An acorn scoop was a handled affair with a loosely woven bottom that could be run along the ground to pick up acorns or nuts. The user could shake the scoop to remove as much dirt and leaves as possible before putting the acorns in the basket.

Acorn-Shaped Basket

For many years, acorns played a strong role in the survival of the Indians. In the early years, despite the bitter taste, acorns were one of the staple foods. When the Indians, especially those in the Northeast, began making items for the tourist trade, they designed and made basketry items that resembled things they saw daily—things that were familiar to them. One of the souvenir pieces was a small basket shaped like an acorn. The slightly pointed ash-splint bottom was dyed green while the sweet-grass top over ash spokes or standards was natural or brown. Credit for the design is usually given

the Passamaquoddies, but more than likely, every basketmaker in the area eventually made them.

Adirondack-Type Baskets

Adirondack is a term used to describe a type of twig or branch furniture made during the first decades of this century. Rather primitive and inexpensive, it was used mostly as lawn furniture or for lake and mountain cabins. Often the bark was left on the branches, which could range in size from quite small to perhaps two inches in diameter. It's not the most attractive furniture in the world, but during the past few years it has experienced a revival in popularity. This, in turn, has sparked a revised interest in baskets made by the same method. The baskets are either used with furniture or are used separately for fruit and flower arrangements.

Adirondack-type basket. 12" sq, 13" o.h. $20–$25

Acorn-shaped basket. 4" h, 4½" dia. $35–$50

Aging New Baskets

Since an old basket is normally priced approximately ten times higher than its new equivalent, it is safe to assume that there will be more artificial aging in the future than there has been in the past. There are those who have been looking to take advantage of this by aging baskets using different processes. This has been going on for a decade or more now, ever since the popularity and prices of old baskets began to soar. Rather than trying to age new baskets, however, some sellers are now opting for paint—inside and out, in never-before-used colors.

It's true that some of the older baskets were painted, usually in the old red, blue, light mustard yellow, and dark green colors. These baskets were probably painted shortly after they were made. Also, some of the old baskets were painted during the past 50 years. They were painted in order to modernize them so they could be used in different settings and not look like work baskets.

During the Depression there was a great surge of painting everything from furniture to baskets. Apparently, money was so scarce, it was simpler and cheaper to paint what one had rather than try to buy something new. The homemaker longing for something new in the home painted both furniture and baskets.

More often than not, older baskets were painted only on the outside. Newly painted ones, however (seen in antique shops, shows, and malls), seem to have been spray-painted in colors like dusty rose, bright yellow, and "sickly" green. They're painted inside and out, without a speck of splint showing, so that one cannot tell if the basket is old or new. This is not aging, but rather covering up the new.

Another way to age new baskets is to hang them outside so they're exposed to both rain and sun. In less than a year, oak splint baskets exposed this way in the Deep South will turn a golden brown—brown enough to pass for an old basket. In the border states of Tennessee and Kentucky, baskets turn a grayish color when left in the sun and rain. Basket-aging experiments in New England have produced a darker basket with black spots resembling mold or maybe soot.

Alaskan Baskets

Most of the Alaskan baskets are made by Eskimos living in the area. See Eskimo.

Amana Colonies

In 1842 a group of German and Swiss immigrants, fleeing their native countries to avoid further religious persecution, came to America, first stopping in New York and finally moved to Iowa around 1855. There they acquired land and built seven self-sufficient villages for 800 residents. Each family had an individual home, but they used a communal kitchen and dining room. Each village had its own shops—a bakery, a blacksmith, a general store, and a basketmaker. Over the years, the basketmakers made a tremendous number of baskets, most of them from willow. Some were made of peeled willow, some unpeeled, and others were a combination of both.

In 1932, the villagers voted to abandon the communal system of living and went their separate ways in the world of free enterprise. Few baskets from this group have since been made, especially baskets for the

The new basket on the left was painted; the small one on the right was "aged" in New England.

public, but there are still a few of the old Amana-made baskets available.

American Balsam Fir

The American balsam fir is a small evergreen of the myrrh family that is used in basketmaking. See "Balm of Gilead."

American Ivy

American ivy is another name for Virginia creeper, a vine used in basketry. See "Virginia Creeper."

Anasazi

Anasazi is a Navajo word meaning "Ancient Ones" that is generally used now to describe the Southwest Indian Basket Maker period, especially the third (last) period.

Animal-Shaped Basketry

Crawfish, Pine Needle

Louisiana has long been famous for its crawfish, so it was only natural that the Coushatta Indians would make a replica of one using pine needles and red raffia. It is very realistic looking and has a small container on the back that qualifies it as basketry. The Coushattas are so skilled in basketry, the 1-inch-by-2-inch lid fits perfectly.

Pine needle effigy of a skunk. $2\frac{3}{4}$" dia, $5\frac{1}{2}$" l including tail. $20–$30

Skunk

Indians have always used the materials available to them and have copied things familiar to them—things they see daily. In the bayou country of southern Louisiana, the Coushattas took pine needles and black and white raffia to fashion a very realistic skunk basket. The lid fits the small opening on top, making this a useful basketry container.

Turtle

Using their skills and experience, the Coushatta made the effigy of a turtle. Using pine needles and raffia, they created a small turtle-shaped container that is unbelievably realistic looking. Like the other animals they make, the turtle has a cover over the storage compartment on its back. Actually, it makes a safe jewelry box, as few thieves would expect to find jewelry in a pine needle container shaped like a turtle.

Pine needle and raffia turtle. $2\frac{3}{4}$" w, $4\frac{1}{2}$" l, 2" h. $15–$24

Pine needle crawfish. 9" l, $2\frac{1}{4}$" w. $18–$35

9

Appalachian Baskets

Actually, few—if any—baskets are known strictly as *Appalachian baskets;* instead, they're usually referred to as baskets made in that area. Mountain people and Cherokee Indians both made a tremendous number of oak, hickory-splint, and river-cane baskets. In fact, they're still making them. Both old and newly made baskets are quite popular now, and prices are high.

Well-made Appalachian splint basket. $275–$425

Small mountain-made egg basket. $250–$400

Round oak-splint work basket. $165–$275

Well-made oak-splint basket. Slight damage, $175–$300.

The most sought after and the most expensive are the so-called egg baskets in the gizzard or buttocks shape. Generally, plain and serviceable baskets like the round and square work and field baskets were made, although quite a few fancy baskets—those made with splints or cane, or dyed with vegetal dyes to form fancy designs—were also produced. Some makers chose to carve fancy handles on otherwise plain baskets.

Mountaineers are known for making more serviceable baskets, while the Cher-

Open Cherokee river-cane basket, approximately 50 years old. $500–$900

Apple Basket

Baskets of one type or another have always been used to gather apples, whether from only a few trees or from an entire orchard. Wire baskets or factory-made wooden splint baskets have been used, as well as baskets woven to fit the needs of the pickers. Many of the fruit-gathering baskets, especially apple and peach baskets, have raised centers in order to prevent undue weight on the apples in the center. Some of the specially made apple baskets were designed oblong with a handle on one side only. This design would allow the basket to be tipped forward so the apples could roll out slowly and easily, thereby preventing as many bruises as possible.

One-handled oak-splint basket. 15" w, 24" l, 16" h. $65–$95

Open Cherokee river-cane basket, 50 years old. $800–$1100

okees are noted for fancy baskets with colorful designs. Both the settlers and Cherokees made baskets from different types of vines, but it appears that the Indians made the majority of them.

Factory-made apple picking-and-storing baskets in half-bushel and bushel sizes. Half-bushel, $45–$60; bushel, $65–$75.

Factory-made apple basket with wooden handles. $55–$85

Apple-Drying Basket

Almost from the very beginning, newcomers to America depended on corn and apples to survive. They had been advised not to drink the water so they drank apple cider. This made apples even more important. When they began to harvest bountiful supplies, they devised other ways of using and preserving them. The winters could be long and hard, so they tried to save as much food from the summer and fall harvest as possible.

One of the things they could do was dry some of the apples. Some people peeled the apples to be dried and others didn't, but everybody sliced the apples and put them in a drying basket where they were left until sufficiently dried. The drying baskets could be square or oblong and with or without handles, but they all had an open-weave bottom to allow air to circulate.

Since few people dry apples anymore, the need for apple-drying baskets no longer exists, but they are very collectible. Perhaps they're more collectible for nostalgia than for decorative purposes.

Art Deco

Prior to the 1920s, the majority of baskets had been made by hand. Of course, several basket factories had been making plain burden baskets as well as some little fruit and nut baskets for years, but the trend was beginning to change. In the 1920s, a few decorative factory-made baskets began to come onto the market. Whereas the older baskets had generally been more utilitarian, these new baskets were being introduced for use in the home to hold fruit or freshly cut flowers. Some were so attractive they were used alone; others were used with wicker furniture just as they are today.

A stain from apples can still be seen in the bottom of this apple-drying basket. 13½" w, 24½" l. $175–$200

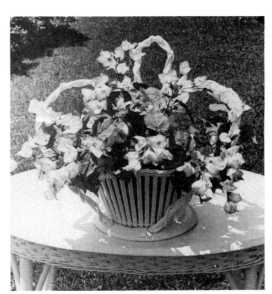

Art Deco basket filled with flowers. 9" w, 17" o.h. $40–$65

Ash Splints

Without ash splints, the Indians of the Northeast couldn't have made the beautiful baskets for which they are so famous. But there is still some controversy over the type of ash used—the black, the brown, or the white.

Some basketmakers claim the black and brown are the same. There are others who claim there is only one variety of ash—it all depends on where it grows. But the Indians who have used ash for centuries will argue otherwise. They say that only brown ash is perfect for making their kinds of baskets.

Black ash is too brittle to use in basketry, say the Indians, and white is coarse, stiff, and dries out too quickly—but brown is perfect. It's not only tough, it is also slow-drying and very flexible. It can also be divided easily into desired widths and thicknesses, which is essential for Northeastern basketmakers, as they only use paper-thin splints in their baskets. It must also be very flexible so that it can be bent and twisted to make all the curly designs.

Ash splints were more widely used than other splint varieties; either that, or more baskets made of ash splints have survived

An ash log cut to size with coil of ash splints on the side.

than those made of other splints. Perhaps one of the reasons for the abundance of ash-splint baskets is that these basketmakers continued working long after the oak and hickory basketmakers of the Southern Highlands and the Ozarks had dwindled to only a few.

It was the custom among most tribes for the men to go into the forest where they selected and cut ash trees perfect for basketry. Years of experience taught them the type of tree to look for and the areas where they would most likely be found. One Penobscot Indian man, who has been gathering ash for basketmaking for half a century, says the best ash trees are almost impossible to find now.

Finding the trees and cutting and fetching them home was only part of the chore. Once home, they had to be cut into sections, and then beaten until the annual growth separated. Instead of having to be split or rived like oak, hickory, or elm, ash will separate simply by being pounded with a maul or mallet. It seems that nature and the ash tree are in cooperation with basketmakers as the annual growth, or layers, of ash trees are nearly perfect in size for making the heavier work baskets. For the small fancy baskets with all types of curlicues, the ash tree layers can be divided and subdivided to make paper-thin splints.

Indians were not the only ones to make ash-splint baskets. Soon after arriving in the new land, the white settlers, too, began to make ash-splint baskets for chores around the home and farm. By sharing ideas, old Americans and new Americans were soon making some of the finest baskets in the world.

Basketmakers like working with ash because it is resistant to decay: You seldom see an ash basket with its bottom rotted away like an oak or hickory basket.

The brown heartwood of the ash was sometimes mixed with the lighter splints from the outside of the tree for a pleasant contrast. Other times, basketmakers would make a few baskets using all-brown heartwood, as they didn't like to waste the hard-to-gather splints. This gave the newly made basket the appearance of an old one.

Ash splints may be plaited or woven freehand, or they may be fitted over a mold or form while still green and pliable. Handles on the work, or burden, baskets were generally made of white ash, while most of the handles on the fancy baskets were plaited out of sweet grass. Sweet grass and Hong Kong grass were mixed with many of the smaller ash-splint baskets. Viburum and other flexible woods were and still are used in some of the ash-splint baskets, and it is not unusual to find them laced around the top with basswood, thin roots of spruce or tamarack, or pumpkin vine.

Asparagus Basket

Every basketmaker worthy of the name has, at one time or another, designed and created special baskets to accommodate special chores. But it is believed that only the Taconics (bushwhackers) made baskets for gathering asparagus.

Asparagus baskets were made of ash or oak and had swing handles. The swing handle was tall enough for the freshly cut asparagus to be slipped into the basket while the basket remained on the gatherer's arm. The basket was wide enough and long enough to accommodate the spears and was also rather shallow, which prevented too much asparagus from being packed in one basket. Asparagus baskets are quite scarce now and are bringing high prices, especially in the Northeast, where collectors are familiar with them.

Woven ash-splint asparagus basket made by the Taconics (bushwhackers) in upper New York State. Approximately 8" w, 15" l, 14" o.h. $200–$400

Authentication

Authentication—confirming what an old basket is made of, where it was made, and by whom—is one of the most difficult chores in basketry. Studying and comparing the work of various people in different areas does help it become easier. Another source of assistance can be the many descendants of the old basketmakers who are still making baskets using the methods of their ancestors.

For instance, the Choctaws in Mississippi and the Chitimachas in Louisiana have always used swamp cane or river cane in their basketmaking. The Cherokees also use it, but not as exclusively as the Choctaws and the Chitimachas. The Choctaws and Cherokees use less color (or less vivid colors) than the Chitimachas. The Cherokees also make oak and hickory split baskets, as well as a wide variety of vine baskets, as did the early settlers of that area and the Ozarks.

With the exception of Chitimacha baskets, both old and new, the old splint baskets made by the North Carolina Cherokees are bringing the best prices today. It's not unusual to find prime examples priced from

$500 to $1500. Their vine baskets, however, are not nearly as popular, nor are they commanding high prices. Prices on their cane baskets range between the splint and vine.

Old Chitimacha baskets are another story, indeed. Owners of old baskets have been offered thousands of dollars for them. The only person known to still be making them is two years behind on orders, and her large baskets are selling for just under $2000.

Mountain-made baskets have always been popular due to the skill and dedication of the makers. The most popular old ones in this category are the splint baskets, which are selling today for prices ranging from $300 to $750. No longer are the poor-quality and damaged ones thrown away; they sell for prices ranging from $25 to $200, depending on quality and condition. Some of the slightly damaged are repaired and put back on the market as good ones.

Not surprisingly, baskets made in a particular area will bring more in that area. This is due, no doubt, to the local collectors' familiarity with the local types of baskets.

Unless you know the history of an item, the authentication and identification of the actual maker is nearly impossible, since any member of the given community could have made the same type basket. This problem is not limited to any specific area of the country.

Some basketmakers had basket shops, while others would have friends join forces to make baskets during the winter—baskets that would be sold in the spring and summer to help augment low salaries or poor farm prices. This approach to making baskets was prevalent with many groups such as the Shaker and Amana colonies of Iowa, and in areas of the country from New England to the Smoky Mountains.

One Indian chief remembers the group he worked with in the 1930s, making 150 baskets each day. They were making them for their roadside stands and tourist and gift shops.

Baskets made by these different groups are similar, almost identical in some cases, and therefore tricky to authenticate by individual maker. Making it even more diffi-

cult is the fact there are no records, and few of the older makers are left.

Dating these baskets is equally as difficult because they were made over such a long period of time. Another problem in dating stems from the fact that new baskets can be left outside for six months to a year to age enough to fool the novice. Aging in the South turns them to a golden brown or beige color, almost the same color as the older baskets. In the mountains, aged baskets turn a sort of aged gray, similar to the older ones found there.

The Miccosukees and Seminoles of Florida and the Coushatta Indians of Louisiana have always been famous for their pine needle baskets, although they still make a few swamp-cane baskets. The Micmac, Penobscot, Passamaquoddy, and Maliseet nations of Maine used predominately ash splint and sweet grass to make their baskets. Other Indian tribes, as well as white basketmakers, used the same materials. This makes it easier to identify the area where the basket was made, but not the maker. The western Indians used yucca, grasses, and rush, along with willow or any other native materials they could find. Indians in the Northwest used plenty of roots and grasses in their baskets.

Most basketmakers have used a variety of materials, including the vines growing in their area. Today, kudzu vine is used. And, to confuse basket collectors even more, an avalanche of baskets are arriving daily, it seems, from China and the Philippines. Few, if any, are made like the old bamboo baskets of a century ago, but the workmanship on them is good and prices are cheap. One organization is having *basket parties* on the order of other home-product parties. All of the party baskets we've seen have had tags specifying that they were for that type of sale and that they were made in the Philippines. All of the party-type baskets appear to be quite well made; in fact, some of them look like cheap versions of the coiled baskets made by the Western Indians.

Basket prices are high now, and seem to be going higher, especially for the good, older baskets. In order to avoid costly mistakes in basketry, it's advisable to learn as much as possible about them before venturing into the marketplace. More information and photos of baskets made by each group can be found under specific headings.

Automobile, Basketry

It has been said that anything can be reproduced in basketry and nearly any material can be used. Apparently that is true, judging from this basketry automobile (see photograph). Nothing is known of its origin, but it appears to date from around 1910–1920. It is definitely fashioned after the cars of that decade, and the maker was very thorough, down to the smallest details. It is made of willow, rattan, and cane. Tacks and brads were used to fasten the strips on the chassis, and large-headed brads were used to make the headlights.

Basketry automobile. 4" w, 9" l, 3½" h. $35–$50

Awls

All basketmakers used an *awl*—a pointed tool for making holes—of one kind or another. Some were made of bone and others from horn, while still another group might prefer to make them from hard oak. Some were even made from the thorns of the thornapple tree. Recently, a basketmaker was seen using an awl made from the handle of an old spoon. Sailors making Nantucket baskets often used awls made of ivory that they found in ports around the world or fashioned from whale's teeth.

Awls like this were necessary to punch holes in the birch bark to make the porcupine quill boxes. Wood awl, $15–$20 (bone awl, $25–$40; ivory awl, $100–$150).

Baby-Related Basketry

Baby Basket

Whether this basket was originally designed as a baby basket or was later found to fit the purpose is probably only known to the first maker. It was and is perfect for the chore and was even more so back in the days when there were no other carriers for babies except maybe a laundry basket.

Oak-splint baby basket. 15½" w, 26½" l, 14½" o.h. $75–$125

16

The baby basket was made of sturdy oak splints that would endure lots of wear and tear. It was large enough so the baby would be comfortable if left in it for several hours. It is believed to have originated in Pennsylvania or Appalachia.

Baby Carrier

In each Indian tribe, a mother would fashion her baby carrier in the manner that best suited her needs: The baby was fastened in the carrier on its mother's back, allowing her to continue working.

Thompson River Indian baby carrier made of the inner bark of cedar, wrapped with grasses. Approximately 25" l. $500–$900

The most beautiful baby carriers were made by the Iroquois and the Thompson River Indians. The workmanship on the old carriers is exquisite. The carrier is a long, beautifully woven basket with buckskin throngs on either end (so the baby could be attached, crosswise, to its mother's back). This was one of the earliest type carriers, and it's possible the babies were later carried in an upright position.

Hupa Baby Basket

From the instant a Hupa Indian baby was born, it was placed in an open-weave basket where it would remain for the next 10 days. Later, the child would have a standing type cradle or carrier that was also carried on the mother's back.

Unlike the later Indian baby carriers, the shallow, round, open-weave carriers are believed to have been used by the Hupa Indians. Baskets were so important to the Hupa, they could actually say they began life in a basket. The Hupa believed that placing a newborn infant in a basket, along with subjecting it to various treatments,

would ward off evil, and the infant's good health would be assured.

It was customary for the grandmother to make both the open-weave baby basket and the cradle the mother would use later. Both were made of peeled shoots of the hazelnut tree. The baby basket was called a *kaitel*.

Baby Scales, Basket

In the 1920s and later, it was the custom to weigh one's baby at home. For this chore, one needed baby scales with a basket so the tiny infant could rest comfortably while being weighed. Manufacturers, always anxious to please the buying public, introduced a variety of baby scales, all with woven, beribboned baskets.

Today, baby-scale baskets aren't used much, but they're part of the basketry and wicker scene and should be saved, if only to complete one's basketry collection.

Baby scales, circa 1920. 13" w, 20" l. $40–$55

Backpacking Baskets

The Indians were using backpacking baskets when the Pilgrims arrived. They used them to move from one location to another. The very early settlers, especially the trappers, soon adapted the Indian's backpacking baskets to their needs. Backpacking baskets are still made today for use by hikers and campers.

Ash-splint backpacking basket with heavy straps, probably made by the Penobscot Indians. 9" by 15" w, 18" h. $65–$95

Backpacking basket with handle to be used when carrying. Has wooden base to prevent wear on splints. $75–$105

Each tribe designed its backpack to suit the tribe's needs. The Micmacs and Penobscots made the finest ones. They're all approximately the same size and in the shape of a medium-sized wastebasket. Others, though, are fancier, with more ornate designs on the corners and around the tops.

Balloon Basket

For the most part, only museums are interested in old balloon baskets, but as the hobby of ballooning continues to grow, so will the demand for new baskets, and there is a chance the older ones will become more popular. They're still being made both here and in England.

Originally, balloon baskets were made of willow, but in recent years, makers in the United States have imported rattan from the Philippines. In England, basketmakers still use the more plentiful willow. It is likely that woven baskets will continue to be used with balloons, since woven materials are lighter than most other material that could

Civil War balloon basket. Army Aviation Museum, Ft. Rucker, Alabama. $800–$1000

be used. Woven baskets are also safe and flexible in case the balloon loses power and lands on or near power lines.

Balm of Gilead

Balm of Gilead is a small evergreen tree of the myrrh family. It's a native of Asia and Africa. In America, the cultivated variety is called American Balsam fir and is grown from Maine to Minnesota. The roots were used to weave baskets that needed heavy bases.

Bamboo

American bamboo is of little use to basketmakers. Most bamboo baskets are made in the Orient from bamboo of the kind that flourishes in the East. It is a treelike tropical plant growing to heights of one hundred feet. (Actually, it is more like a reed than a tree,

Later bamboo drying basket. 21" w, 8" h. $35–$65

but grows so large and tall it becomes tree-like.)

Mature Oriental bamboo stalks can be as wide as six feet in diameter and strong enough to be used in building houses and making furniture and ship masts. The medium-sized stalks are used for canes and basketry, while the young shoots are used for food.

In years past, both the Chinese and Japanese were noted for the rich brown color of their best bamboo baskets. The color was not achieved with dyes, but by searching out old pieces of bamboo from houses being torn down. It mellows to just the right shade from years of use and smoke.

Bangladesh-Made Baskets

New baskets from Bangladesh are being imported into the United States on a regular basis. They are very inexpensive and can be used in many ways (for example, as covers for flower pots). Confusion concerning dating may arise in the future when these baskets have aged, because they are almost identical to those made by the Gullahs in South Carolina. They are also similar to the rye- and wheat-straw baskets made here.

Old brown bamboo basket painted blue. 7¼" dia, 13" h. $20–$35

19

New coiled basket from Bangladesh. 5½" h, 7½" dia. New, $3–$5.

Basket Forms or Molds

Wooden forms over which baskets were woven. See "Forms or Molds for Baskets."

Basket-in-a-Basket

Basket collectors are so oriented to looking for handled baskets that they often miss strange basketry items. That was the case with the four small nested baskets found in an old knotted carrying basket. The knotted carrying basket seems to be a bit older than the nest of baskets although they were found as pictured in an antique shop in Maine.

Four nested baskets in a knotted carrying basket. Largest, 4½" w, 7½" l, 1½" h; smallest, 3" w, 5½" l, 1" h. Set, $15–$20.

They appear to be made of some kind of cane. The purpose for which they were made and used is unknown.

Basketmaker

Basketmaker is a word commonly used to describe anyone who makes baskets, but in the old Indian culture it was used to describe the transitional life of the early Indians of the Southwest. In the beginning, they lived very primitively. The Indians were simply small-game hunters who used primitive spears, snares, and nets. For their other food, they depended on whatever was growing wild in the area, but even for that time (between 1 and 400 A.D.) they are credited with making beautiful baskets. Many of those old baskets have been found and dated by teams who established digs in the area in

Old picture of a basketmaker taking her wares to town.

Oil painting of woman carrying a basket of laundry.

1880. One of the most surprising things about the digs was the number of finer baskets found turned upside down over the faces of the deceased. It's believed archaeologists were the first to use the term *Basket Maker* for the people of that period, and they coined it because of the many exquisite baskets they found in the digs.

Researchers continued to use the word to describe the next period (400 to 700 A.D.) when the Indians of the Southwest moved from Desert Culture to Agriculture. Not a booming agriculture, to be sure, but a beginning. At least they began growing some corn and squash, and maybe other foods. This period is referred to as *Basket Maker II*.

Their lifestyles continued to improve during *anasazi*, the third period (700 to 1100 A.D.); they began to build houses of wattle and daub, wear cotton clothing, and they continued to make baskets of all kinds. Sometime during this period they began observing rich ceremonials that necessitated the use of fine handicrafts, especially ele-

gant items of basketry. There was one exception, the Tarahumaras, who developed a lifestyle much like the first Basket Makers. They continued living that style for centuries.

Basketmaker's Pack Basket

Some basketmakers, especially those who depended only on selling baskets to supplement other income, usually took their baskets to town on horseback, in a buggy or wagon, or on their own backs. For the latter chore, they usually made large baskets similar to the backpacking peat baskets or the later clothes hampers. The baskets had to be as light as possible as they would be piled high with smaller baskets.

Basket with Overlapping Cover

A book on basketmaking was published in 1915 that gave instructions for making a "Basket with Overlapping Cover." This one was made using those instructions. No specific use was given for the basket, but it would have made an excellent sewing basket or costume jewelry basket.

It is made of rattan with two bands of splints around the side with fancy weaving above and below. At one time all the rattan was dyed or washed in a rich green color. It is quite faded around the sides and on the cover, but it is still a rich green inside the basket and the base.

Rattan basket. 9" dia, 6½" h. $12–$23

Basswood

Basswood is used in basketmaking today much as it was a century ago. It can be boiled if toughness is required, but in most cases, the inner bark—after it has been cut into long, thin strips and placed among rushes on the edge of a lake—can be used just as it is, peeled and separated from the outer bark. When necessary, it can be twisted into twine that can be used to weave either mats for the floor or can be used to fasten coiled baskets. Like most of the materials used by the old basketmakers, basswood strips could be gathered, separated, and wrapped into coils to be used when needed.

Inside of basket showing how beads were sewn on.

Beaded Basket

The sight of this basket conjures up visions of the South Sea Islands. Closer inspection shows that a tremendous amount of work was required to sew on all the tiny beads. It also has a round tin insert in the top, which is very unusual, but probably was made to allow the basket to be carried on one's head.

Origin, material, and use are unknown, but the workmanship is superb. Thousands of tiny beads have been handsewn on the bottom and over fabric sewn on first in special places.

Beehives

Long before the introduction of wooden beehives, beekeepers made hives of coiled rye. Those who preferred the rye or straw hives used them for years, probably from habit, but it is known that they continued to use them for years after others were using wooden hives. In fact, some continued to use them until they were outlawed because

Rye beehive. $200–$300

Beaded basket. 10″ dia, 3½″ h. $55–$95

New coiled beehive (skep) from Haiti. Reportedly made of rice grass, but the material is very coarse. Good fragrance. 16" dia, 16" h. $16–$20

it was thought they might harbor diseases harmful to the bees.

Basket beehives were inexpensive, as everyone had rye straw, and they were easy to make. The maker only had to coil enough rye straw to make a hive of the size he or she wanted and then make a small opening in the front for the bees to leave and return. As soon as the maker installed a frame in the bottom to hold the honey, he or she was in business.

This style beehive is believed to have originated with the Pennsylvania Dutch, who called them *skeps*. Old rye beehives are not too plentiful, but new ones, some quite crude, are being made.

Bells

It is little wonder that the history of bells has been lost in the sea of antiquity when we realize they've been used in China for over 46 centuries. During that time, they've been made of nearly every known material, and used in as many different ways.

Rattan bell. 6" dia, 6" h. $5–$10

Christmas bell made by the Senecas. Ash splint and sweet grass. 3" dia, 3" h. New, $6–$8; old, $10–$15.

23

Two Gullah-made bells. Large: 2½" dia, 2" h; small: 2" dia, 1½" h.. $5–$8

Pair of grass bells. Small: 1½" dia, 1¼" h; large: 2" dia, 2" h. $9–$12

So it shouldn't be surprising to find that they were, and still are, being made in basketry. The Gullahs of South Carolina are making small hanging bells of sea grass and palmetto. Bells made of rattan are used at weddings and to hold mistletoe at Christmas.

Belt

Skilled basketmakers have to test themselves occasionally by making something not made before. This was the case of the Stouff family years ago when they not only designed, but made, a double-woven belt. It is made of finely cut strips of swamp cane dyed in bright colors–colors that have faded some through the years. Double weaving requires expertise many basketmakers don't have, and to make a belt requires ingenuity, skill, and patience.

Swamp-cane double-woven belt. $500–$600

Berry Basket

Since the settlers and the Indians depended so much on berries of all kinds, it was only natural that they made special berry-picking

Crudely made bark-berry picking basket. 6" sq, 12" o.h. $18–$25

baskets. Some were made of wooden splints, while others were made of various barks. They were not made to be works of art, but rather primitive baskets that could be taken to the woods and fields with the expectation of berry stains.

Beverage Caddy

Before the advent of movies and television, big entertainment in the home consisted of maybe a dinner party once a week. During the summer both the family and visiting "young folk" were served beverages on the front porch nearly every night. The beverage was usually lemonade.

To make it easier to carry glasses that were full, basketmakers began making bev-erage caddies. The first ones were made around 1915, but they remained popular until the 1950s. The plywood bases were used to make them stronger.

Bikahlagenigan

Bikahlagenigan is the Penobscot name for the crooked knife used by most basketmakers. It's one of the essential tools in basketry. The Penobscots call the regular knife *sekwak* (the plural is *sekwagol*). There is little demand for the knives today, as most basketmakers have their own. Studying the knives helps collectors understand how the old baskets were made.

Rattan beverage caddy. $10–$15

Gullah-made beverage caddy. $12–$17

Crooked knife or bikahlagenigan *with a basket. Basket, $50–$75; bikahlagenigan, $40–$50.*

Big Basket–Little Basket

No logical answer has been found to explain why anyone would make a basket like this. It was found a quarter of a century ago at an estate sale in the hills of eastern Tennessee. Only the maker knew why he or she needed this type basket, but it is a good example of the strange shapes and designs that were used.

Birch-bark basket with scalloped top. 6" h, 7" dia. $25–$40

Oak-splint basket with smaller one on the side. Large: 13" dia, 10" h; small: 6" dia, 4½" h. $75–$125

Birch Bark

The bark of the birch tree was used for many things. The white settlers soon learned from the Indians that it could be used to make everything from canoes to baskets. Birch bark was used to make dishes, funnels, cooking utensils, fans, covering for dwellings, and *makuks* (a primitive but useful container that might be used for storing food, maple syrup, or water—if the seams were waterproof).

The reason for birch bark's popularity and usefulness was its abundance and its variety of thicknesses. For instance, the heaviest bark from large trees might have six to nine distinct layers and be strong enough to make a large canoe. On other trees, the bark was almost paper thin, but still strong enough to hold light items like food.

Birch-bark basket, applied design; new. $65–$95

Birch-bark baskets and other items made from the bark often split with age. But the splits were easily mended using the gum from the balsam. This feature was very attractive to the women whose baskets might split while they were out gathering berries—they could mend the baskets quickly and resume berry gathering.

Covered birch-bark etched design basket. 4½" w, 3½" h. $30–$65

Side of porcupine quill–decorated birch-bark box, 2½" h, 3½" w. Unity College collection. $100–$150

Birch-bark baskets range from crude, vine-handled berry baskets to more sophisticated examples with beautiful etched designs on the sides. Some were made of lighter bark and trimmed with darker bark.

Birch bark was, and still is, used as the foundation for porcupine quill boxes and baskets. The quills are fastened to the top layer of birch, then lined with another layer so the quills will be covered. All this is fastened together with spruce roots or basswood. Moose-hair embroidery was also done on birch bark, as well as on leather.

Birch-bark box with moose-hair embroidery. Unity College collection. $250–$300

Bird Nest

Bird nests were one of the easiest basketry items to make, but today few are available. Perhaps large numbers were made and left in the trees to deteriorate.

Apparently, the idea originated at the

Old picture of a basketry bird nest. $20–$25

27

Bird Market in Paris where they were sold in large numbers around the turn of the century. An important rule in making bird nests was to make them as inconspicuous as possible—birds like nests that are natural looking. Suggested materials for making them were willow, twigs, and grasses, or they could be made of the same materials—twig spokes and rush weavers—as those sold at the Paris Bird Market.

Bishop, Ralph

Contemporary Maine basketmaker, and the only white man known to still be making porcupine quill baskets.

Block Printing

Originally, designs were painted on baskets in a freehand or geometric design. Later, for those unable to make the simple designs, or for those preferring an easier method, block printing (also called potato printing) was devised. Indications are that this type decoration originated with the Algonkian tribes.

Basket with block printing. 15" h, 20" dia. $200–$350

For block or potato printing, a basketmaker would cut a design on a potato or block of wood. Next, the design would be dipped into a plant stain or other dyes before applying it to the spokes or weavers.

Open basket with wide and narrow ash splints block printed. 15" sq, 7" h. $95–$175

Covered ash-splint basket with block printing. 12" w, 24" l, 12" h. $150–$250

Bloodroot

The inner bark of the roots of this plant was used to make a red or orange dye, depending on how it was used. A century ago, Indians used a handful of bloodroot mixed with a handful of wild plums in a quart of hot water to make a deep red that was said to make an excellent dye for porcupine quills—quills that would later be used to decorate boxes and baskets. Fresh bloodroot rubbed on wooden splints produces an orangey shade.

Blueberries

Blueberries were used to make a reddish-pink dye for use in basketry. Also see "Red Dye."

Bone

The term *bone* in basketmaking refers to the awl-like instrument used by the Gullah basketmakers of South Carolina. The first ones were made of bone, hence the name, but more recently the Gullah are making them from old spoon handles.

Bonnet Basket

Some believe these popular baskets originated in New Hampshire, but it's a well-known fact that they were made all over New England. Many feel these baskets were made by both settlers and Indians, but most of the baskets were probably made by the Indians and sold to the settlers.

Some were square based with round covers, indicating they had some difficulty converting the basket's original square form to a round shape. But that skill was mastered, and bonnet baskets were eventually made in all shapes.

For home use they were large enough

Penobscot-made bonnet basket of ash splints. **$150–$200**

Ash-splint bonnet basket made by the Penobscot Indians. 20" dia, 16" h. **$15–$265**

Ash-splint bonnet basket with block printing. 15" h, 20" dia. **$200–$300**

Late Indian-made ash and sweet-grass bonnet basket. Unity College collection. **$90–$175**

29

to hold quite a bit of clothing or several bonnets at one time. This was a time when storage containers and storage space was at a premium. They were low enough to be stored under the high beds, and they were also a popular substitute for the hat or band-box when traveling by stagecoach or packet.

Earlier examples have been seen covered with chintz and are round at the bottom with a drawstring at the top. The cover served a dual role—it kept dust out of the clothing and bonnets, and it kept the basket clean and new-looking. In fact, one will be seen from time to time that looks almost new, and chances are it was kept covered, or maybe put in the attic long after it was no longer used.

Most of the bonnet baskets were made of rather wide ash splints, not cut too thin so the baskets would be sturdy and serviceable. Many have potato or block printing. Bonnet baskets seem to have originated around the late 1700s, and their popularity continued until around 1860—and even later in some areas.

Bookmarks

During the early part of this century (about 1913 to 1929), a period in basketry that could rightfully be called the Souvenir Age, both Indians and whites in the Northeast made any and everything they thought the visiting tourist would buy. Some of the easiest and less expensive items to make were the ash-splint and sweet-grass bookmarks. They were easily made from the leftovers of other projects. At five cents each, bookmarks were priced so a family could afford a dozen or more.

Orange and yellow ash-splint and sweet-grass bookmarks. 8″ and 10″ h, 2½″ dia. $8–$15

Boston Ivy

In basketry the larger vines of Boston ivy can be used as spokes while the smaller ones are split to make fine weavers. Examples are hard to find, and even harder to authenticate unless, of course, one is a botanist.

Bottle Basket

When all beverages from milk to wine were bottled in glass and there were no metal carriers, basketmakers came to the rescue. They made four- and six-compartment baskets to accommodate the breakable bottles. Some were made with movable partitions that could be arranged to fit different size

Four-compartment willow bottle basket. 10" sq, 14" o.h. $25–$35

bottles. Others had stationary partitions. Generally, they were made of willow. Since the popularity of baskets in general has been escalating, bottle baskets are again being made; in fact, nearly all types of baskets are being made today.

Bottle, Basketry-Covered

Basketry-covered bottles and jugs made in the 1800s could be any size from a pint to a gallon, but most were in the quart to half-gallon sizes. The basketry covers might be made of willow or oak splints, depending on what the company wanted.

Reports indicate that both whites and Indians were employed to make the covers. In the Northeast, they were often made of ash splints. The basketry covers were used to protect the glass bottle (often brown) from breakage in shipping. Handles were added to make it easier to take the bottle or jug back for a refill. The making of basketry-covered bottles and jugs ceased nearly a

century ago in the States, but various types of alcoholic beverages were bottled in basketry-covered containers until the 1970s. Most of the more recent covers were made in Italy.

Old basketry-covered wine bottle from Spain with woven cover over cork. 12½" h. $10–$12

Brown half-gallon jug in basketry. From New York. $18–$30

Bottoms of Baskets

The bottom of a basket is often a clue to the skills of the maker and the sturdiness and lasting quality of the basket. Some baskets have a reinforced bottom with exposed spokes. Others, like some of the large storage baskets, have a rim woven halfway between the center and the outside, while still others will have a wide splint around the outside of the bottom. Then there are baskets with extra weavers or spokes added to each corner that extend down to form short legs. On a loosely woven bottom, this would allow air to circulate more freely. Baskets were made with runner-type splints on the bottom. The runners not only protected the bottom, but they also could be used to slide the basket along without damaging the splint bottom.

Passamaquoddy-made basketry cover of sweet grass and ash splints. 9" h, 2" dia bottom, ¾" dia top. $25–$35

Raised woven ring on bottom of basket.

Reinforced bottom.

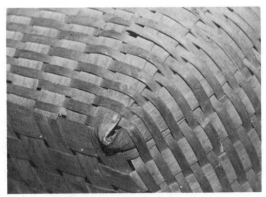

Extra spokes were added on each corner to form legs.

Heavy rim on bottom of round basket.

Bracelet Baskets

Whether or not these tiny baskets were ever worn on bracelets is unknown. If they were, it was probably to advertise the maker's wares. They were used occasionally to decorate other pieces of basketry. The Penobscots, Malisetts, and Pasamaquoddies were among the most prolific makers of bracelet baskets, while the Micmacs only made a few. Other basketmakers may have made them as well.

Tiny bracelet basket. ¾" dia, 1½" o.h. $8–$12

Bracken

Bracken refers to any number of large, coarse ferns whose roots were gathered, cleaned, and split to be used in basketry. Bracken was especially useful in making dark patterns.

Braiding

See "Plaiting."

Brass Baskets

Many different materials have been used to make baskets. Some have worked well, others not so well. The materials that worked were used repeatedly while the others were not. Brass is a metal, and it apparently didn't work well in basketry, although it has been used to make some small, decorative baskets.

Brass basket. 5½" l, 3" o.h. $7–$12

Bread-Raising Baskets

The German immigrants who settled in Pennsylvania are believed to be the first to make dough- or bread-raising baskets. Whether or not they were the first doesn't matter when you consider the large number they made. These baskets, usually called *Mennonite* baskets, were usually made of rye.

Other basketmakers, using whatever materials were available, produced some bread-raising baskets of coiled-wrapped straw. In the early days, these baskets were used exclusively for bread raising. After the introduction of tin and graniteware bread raisers, these baskets might have been used for many household chores.

Bread-raising basket. 14" dia, 5½" h. $35–$70

Bread-Serving Baskets

Like all other baskets, those for serving bread came in a variety of shapes, but none was quite as popular as oblong. Bread baskets can be used to serve rolls, a loaf of bread, slices of bread, and even crackers. Most were made of willow and were made by both the white and the Indian basketmakers.

Oblong willow bread tray. 6" w, 12" l, 4½" h.
$9–$17

Bromegrass

In checking the various grasses used in basketmaking, we found there were at least a half dozen species of each, with different ones growing in different areas. This meant the basketmaker used the variety that was most convenient. But then basketmakers were never too concerned with species or botanical names; they called all the materials by the common names used in their area. In this case, *brome* was derived from the Greek *bormos,* a kind of oat. None of the species of bromegrass was eaten by cattle or horses because it was too tough, but the split stems were used to an advantage in basketry—to make a white design in split-root baskets.

Brown Jar, Basketry-Covered

Several things came in brown jars during the first decades of this century, but the item most often found was snuff. Many women saved and found alternative uses for these jars rather than discarding them. They were often used for canned fruits and vegetables.

Brown jar covered with ash splints and Hong Kong grass. 3¼" dia, 6" h. $17–$25

Today the jars are collected as advertising items since they have the information about the snuff companies on the sides and the lids. Apparently, covering a brown jar with basketry was not only a way to save it, but a challenge.

Buck Basket

Buck basket is the term used in some parts of the country to mean "laundry basket." It originated from the word *buck,* which described lye or soapsuds used to wash clothes.

Bushel Baskets

Bushel baskets were the backbone of the farm as well as the grocery store. They were large enough and strong enough to carry large loads to and from the fields, and their size and strength was an advantage for the country storekeeper who used them for dis-

Taconic bushel basket dating from around 1920. $400–$700

Bushel basket with reinforced bottom. 20" dia, 15" h. $235–$350

Close-up of handles on Taconic bushel basket.

Handmade oak-splint buck or laundry basket. 23" w, 27" l. $50–$75

Factory-made oak-splint buck or laundry basket. 19" w, 29" l. $25–$40

playing heavy produce and maybe for delivering.

As a general rule, men made the bushel baskets; this seems to have been especially true of the so-called bushwacker basketmakers. The reason for this was the fact the splints, whether ash, oak, hickory, or maple, had to be thicker than those used in the smaller baskets, which meant they were harder to weave and required a stronger basketmaker.

Because bushel baskets were made and used for heavier loads, the handles were made stronger and positioned to carry extra weight. Bushel baskets are not as sought after today as other baskets due to the fact that they are harder to use and take up lots of space.

Taghkanic (or Taconic) baskets will be

found more easily in New York State where they were made. In the heyday of the manufacture of these baskets, basketmakers are known to have taken loads of the baskets around New England where they were sold.

Bushwhacker Baskets

It's physically impossible to identify every old basket with its maker. But as more and more research is done, the history of many baskets is surfacing.

For years, numerous sturdy baskets could be found, but they defied authentication. They were usually referred to as "Shaker" or "Shaker-type." Then, two basket researchers found they had been made by some very skilled basketmakers in the village of Taghkanic, New York. The researchers, Martha Wetherbee and Nathan Taylor, found the people had been living in the mountains for centuries making and selling their baskets. They became known as *bushwhackers,* a name that was to imply they didn't know how to do anything other than live in the hills, marry each other, and make baskets.

These baskets are also known as *Taconic* baskets because the name of the village has since been simplified to Taconic.

But whatever the name, they are some of the finest authenticated baskets in the country. Once the genuine baskets have been studied, they are more easily recognized. All of the baskets are made of ash and oak splints, and the most desirable ones have round tops and bottoms, and swing handles.

Bushwhacker baskets were made by the thousands during the years they were made so prolifically. Like so many other basketmakers, these people made baskets all winter to be sold in the spring and summer, and like the others, they suffered a loss of income when the paper bag replaced the basket.

Butterweed

A wild flower with a yellow daisylike blossom that was used to make yellow dye. Grown abundantly in Louisiana and maybe in other areas as well. Also called *yellow top.*

Buttocks Baskets

For years this type basket, with the center rib or spoke indented so that it resembled both a gizzard and the buttocks, was known primarily as a *gizzard basket,* especially in the mountains of Tennessee and Kentucky

Bushwhacker basket. 18" dia, 13" h. $300–$500

Fancy oak-splint buttocks basket. Note extra rim on top weaving and design on handle going under the basket. 12" dia, 14" o.h. $350–$500

Small oak-splint buttocks basket. 6½" dia, 7" h. Some damage. $85–$250, depending on amount of damage.

Small oak-splint buttocks basket. 7½" dia, 6" h. $200–$350

Finely woven buttocks basket with well-worn handle. 10½" dia, 13" h. $250–$400

where so many were made. Then it began to be called a *buttocks basket,* which is the English translation of the Pennsylvania Dutch term describing the basket's resemblance to the human derriere. Then somebody with a sense of humor and rhyme began calling them "Granny's Fanny" baskets.

The name-calling didn't stop there. Some of the mountaineers who made them called them "hip baskets," probably because of the shape which allowed them to be carried easily and comfortably on the hip. Since some mountaineers had to carry eggs to the store to sell or trade, which could

be a long walk, they were very conscious of anything that distributed the weight and made it easier to carry the burden.

This type basket has also been known as a "pack basket" and a "saddle basket," because it rode along easily when tied on the saddle horn. "Bow basket" is still another name that crops up. There is still a chance you will hear them called by one of these names, depending on what part of the country you are in. They were made in a variety of styles and sizes. They seem to be more popular now in the South and Midwest than in the Northeast and Southwest.

Button Baskets

Cherokee

At one time or another almost every basketmaker made button baskets, or at least, if not actually given that name, small baskets that could be used for buttons. They were handy little gadgets for the housewife with a large family who was constantly replacing buttons.

This button basket (see photograph) is made with small oak splints and honeysuckle vine and dyed with bloodroot and walnut to give it the orange and brown colors.

Button basket made by the Cherokees. 4" dia, 4" h. $20–$30

Sweet Grass

Most of the small button baskets made by the Indians of New England were made more for souvenirs than as serviceable items, although they would hold several buttons. They are made of finely cut splints of ash and sweet grass. Dyed rows alternated with natural, and some of the colors were bright in the later pieces.

Souvenir sweet-grass button basket. 2" dia, 1½" h. $15–$23

Cajun Baskets

The Cajuns of Louisiana were excellent basketmakers, but there is little demand for their baskets today. A few makers still weave the old oak-splint baskets, but the paper bag and box have all but eliminated the need for baskets. In earlier years they made rice baskets, but now the rice is harvested with machines.

New Cajun-made oak-splint basket. 17" dia, 8" h. $26–$40

Cake Baskets

Years ago, there were very few bakeries. Housewives were proud of their culinary skills and couldn't resist the temptation to take a freshly baked cake to every social event. For the baked goods to arrive in perfect condition, they needed to be transported in special cake carriers. Manufacturers heard the cry, and answered with cake baskets in silver, porcelain, and glass. Basketmakers also became aware of the trend and made less expensive models in every material, from oak splints to coiled pine needles.

In the days before so many women went into the work force, women entertained frequently at home. The entertaining might consist of a large family dinner, or it could be afternoon tea. Afternoon tea was the custom in England, and when they came to America, many of the English brought the custom with them.

Rattan cake basket. 10" dia, 9" h. $27–$39

Round oak-splint cake basket. $150–$225

Square oak-splint cake basket. $175–$250

The home and its furnishings were of utmost importance to the Victorian ladies, as each was judged by her peers on the condition and appearance of her home—and the way she entertained. In the mountain areas of Tennessee, homemakers seemed to opt for oak-splint cake baskets, but in the Northeast, it was ash and sweet grass.

Candy Basket

Dozens of variations of this rattan basket were made from instructions given in the basketry books published nearly a century ago, and they were all called *candy baskets*. These are the same baskets you see so often holding yarn in the "country home" pictures. Loosely woven versions of the candy basket are the most available. They vary in size from 7 to 13 inches in diameter, and 2 to 5 inches in height. Prices vary from $2 at a barn or garage sale to as much as $15 at antique shows. Some are natural and others are stained a dark brown, but most have been painted white.

White rattan candy basket. 10" dia, 3" h. $10–$15

Candy Boxes, Grass

While searching for information on the raffia-wrapped grass boxes that are so often called Shaker but are not, we heard that some of these boxes had labels from candy companies. After two years of searching one was finally found. It lists the maker as F. H. Roberts Co., Boston, maker of The Appollo Chocolates.

Query letters were sent to several places in Boston, but no replies were received. There may not be any specific information on the maker and the boxes, but the photograph proves they were used to package candies.

Raffia-wrapped, grass candy box with candy company card on top. $2\frac{1}{2}''$ w, 6" l, 2" h. $20–$33

Cane, Swamp or River

A number of plants, similar to bamboo, that have long, willowy, reedlike stalks are called *cane*. The word *cane* is used frequently by basket collectors, but among basketmakers, it's identified by the area where it is grown.

The Cherokees and mountain basketmakers call it *river cane,* while the Mississippi and Louisiana Indians call it *swamp cane.* In the mountain areas it is generally found along the river banks. One Choctaw basketmaker said she had to travel as far as two miles into the swamps to find good cane. What she finally found and cut had to be carried out the same way she came in—on foot.

In Louisiana, the Chitimachas go along the bayous to find the best canebrakes

Cane from the first split.

(thickets). In the best canebrakes, cane grows close together, the air is hot and sticky, and the area is filled with mosquitos. And, wherever there is cane, there is danger of snakes—no better place does the canebrake rattler thrive than in the bayous. But cane basketmakers will go where necessary to get the best cane—long, straight stalks with long joints—for their baskets.

Gathering and preparing any basket materials can be a long, drawn-out process, but cane is the most time-consuming of all. It has to be gathered—and in the case of the Choctaws, carried a couple of miles through the swamps—and then it must be kept damp until it can be split. The first split is made by notching one end of the round stalk with a sharp knife. The strips are split and split again until they are all less than a half-inch wide each. Actually, they are each only a bit wider than one-fourth of an inch. The outside layer is held in the teeth and peeled with the hands to remove the pithy center. For the next two weeks, the strips are left outside for dew to fall on them. During that time, the cane strips will lose their natural green color and turn a soft golden brown.

For those who want even finer strips, the cane strips may be split once again. Either way, once they've reached the golden brown color, they are ready to be dyed or used as is.

Three canteens with woven grass covers. Bottle is 8" h, 5½" w. **$10–$15 each**

Canteen

The origin of these woven grass-covered canteens is unknown. An antique dealer bought them at an estate auction in New England but was unable to get any historical information about them. Their tops are stoppers rather than screw-on lids, and their shape is similar to some of the old wine bottles, but there is no explanation for the long shoulder straps unless they were to be taken on hiking trips. The covers are not woven on the bottles as are other kinds; instead, they are attached in three pieces—one on either side and another on the bottom. The seams are covered with a heavy twill-type material and resemble braids; they are hand sewn. The straps or cords are fastened with hand-stitching near the top.

Card Case

It is doubtful that anything under the sun escaped the basketmakers. Naturally, splints were too wide and too stiff to make card cases, so they used grass, the same type grass that was used to make the wallets. The

Woven grass card case, probably made in the Orient. 2¼" w, 4" h. **$6–$9**

card case also has a liner made out of palm leaves. It would protect the fragile, woven case. The grass was dyed a winey red, green, and yellow.

Carpet Beater

It seems a bit strange to classify carpet beaters as baskets until you remember that instructions for making them are found in basketry books. Oldtimers made them, if they needed them, without instructions or measurements. They simply looped a few branches of willow or other tough vine, wrapped the handle, and they were in business. The books give specific instructions along with exact measurements.

Cat Basket

Another late bloomer in the basketry field, cat baskets, were made in two styles: the covered basket shown in the photograph and the open basket type that resembles a small, oblong laundry basket. These baskets probably date from around the same period as the cat carrier and were still being made a few years ago. So many basketry items are made in China and the Philippines, it is possible they are still being made. Traditionally, a pillow was placed in the bottom of the basket, and the basket was usually kept in the room in which the family spent most of its leisure time. Some cat baskets have been painted white and now hold fuzzy toy kittens.

Willow carpet beater. 7½" w, 25½" l. $18–$32

White cat basket. 16" h, 16" w. $25–$30

43

Cat Carrier

Cat carriers are also late bloomers. It's very possible some of the early basketmakers had cats they treasured and so made carriers for them, but the photograph shown here is one of the oldest we've seen. Prior to the last half century, cats were not usually house pets, but rather lived around the barn and outside buildings. It is only recently that owners began taking their cats on trips that would require a cat carrier.

Willow cat carrier with lightweight iron door. $58–$70

Cat's Head Basket

The Shakers made a style of basket that was called a *cat's head basket* because the bottom of the basket resembles the head of a cat. See "Shaker Baskets."

Cattails

A cattail is a tall reedlike marsh plant with long leaves and a brown, fuzzy, cylindrical flower. The stalks are used in basketry.

Gatherers who aren't too familiar with different plants often confuse rush, flag, and cattails, but all will work well in basketry. All three are found in moist places, from marshes and lowlands to the banks of sluggish streams.

Some species of cattail grow as high as 8 to 10 feet tall, while the majority only attain heights of 4 to 5 feet. The taller cattails are more desirable for basketmaking. The color and texture of cattails will vary from one stream to another and from one part of the country to another, indicating that their different appearances are dependent, somewhat, on the type of soil found in the marshes.

Cattail, like cane, can be split and dyed for basketmaking and, when mixed with cane, can be mistaken for cane.

Cedar

Both the roots and bark of cedar have been used in basketry. Cedar roots have been used for years, and some baskets made from them are watertight, provided the weaving and twining is tight enough. Split fibrous cedar roots were used for many types of basketry—the Wampanoags used them to a great advantage, making eel traps. They would split the long cedar roots and wrap them with smaller ones. The bark of red cedar was also used in basketry, to make pack or flat baskets.

Mention cedar and the average person thinks of a cedar chest or a closet lined with cedar—it is supposed to inhibit moths and other insects that attack clothing. However, cedar reached an earlier popularity as basket material.

Cemetery Flower Baskets

Half a century or so ago, cemetery arrangements were made from fresh flowers usually cut from one's own garden. These were arranged in poorly woven, inexpensive baskets with metal containers. Florists used the same type baskets. Some families would leave the baskets on graves and put fresh

White cemetery flower basket. 15" dia, 35" o.h.
$10–$15

Basket of the type used at funerals and at home to hold cut flowers. $9–$20

flowers in them from time to time. A few families would even use these baskets at home to hold fresh flowers. When a newer or better container was found, the old ones were discarded or relegated to the attic. Cemetery flower baskets were usually sprayed in colors with a touch of gold and were attractive containers.

Chatelaine

Chatelaine is French for "lady of the castle," or "mistress of the chateau." It is also the word for a long waist chain with a pendant clasp, that ladies wore years ago to hold their purses, keys, and other valuables.

With the passing of time, customs changed, and by the time Victorian ladies began designing chatelaines, they dispensed with the long waist chain. Long waist chains were replaced with a simpler chatelaine, one that fastened on the waistband of a skirt or dress. The later chatelaines were generally made of sterling silver, although a few plated ones were made. Several silver chains were fastened to the waistband plate, and each of these chains had a swivel end from which hung scissors, keys, needlecases, a pencil, and maybe a penknife and scent bottle.

When the Indians and whites of the Northeast began making basketry items for tourists, they copied old ideas they thought would sell. One of those was the chatelaine which they made of sweet grass and finely cut ash splints. Their version, held together with ribbon, included a booklet filled with flannel, for needles; a small basket for spools of thread; a woven velvet-covered sweet-grass pin cushion; a thimble holder; and a small case for scissors. These sweet-grass and ash-splint chatelaines probably were not used in the same manner as the original chatelaine. Housewives would hang them on their walls in order to easily find their sewing tools, rather than wearing them.

The Penobscot and Passamaquoddy Indians were the most prolific makers of chatelaines, and either they, or others, made a variation—a disc with a thread basket, thimble, and scissors holder.

Woven disc with metal thimble and no scissors. $38–$60

Cheese Basket

Less than a century ago, nearly every family in the country owned a cow. They used the excess milk to make butter and cheese. Making the butter wasn't such a big chore, but making cheese was a long, drawn-out process. First, the milk had to be left in a warm place until it soured and formed curds. The cheese basket (usually a hexagon-weave basket) was lined with cloth, filled with the curds, and placed on a rack over a vat that would catch the dripping whey. Later the

Sweet-grass and ash-splint chatelaine with sterling thimble and scissors. $85–$115

Hexagon-shaped cheese basket. 22" dia, 5" h. $350–$500

Ash-splint compote.

Navajo wedding basket.

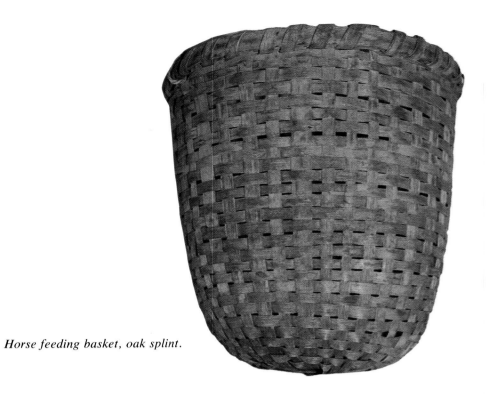

Horse feeding basket, oak splint.

Corn- or hominy-washing basket made by Se-neca Indians.

Baby basket.

Buttocks baskets and late swing-handle, painted blue.

Apples in hand basket.

Woven Chinese zhen (or chen) pillow or head-rest.

Apples in contemporary swing-handle basket.

Prison-made basket after the Nantucket style.

Strawberry-shaped basket made of ash splints.

Ash-splint doll cradle, probably Passama-quoddy-made.

Contemporary swing-handle basket with dried arrangement.

Dried arrangement in hand basket.

Ash-splint scale basket.

Ash-splint basket after the Shaker style.

Round cheese basket with hexagon weave. 22" dia, 4" h. $350–$450

curds were put into a cheese mold, and in due time, the family had homemade cheese.

Cheese Mold

Every effort was made to find out why an antique dealer in a New Hampshire mall labeled this basket a "cheese mold." We were unable to find the owner, and the mall manager didn't know. Others who might have known were queried, but no one could vouch for its authenticity. Several thought it could be a small mold, just large enough for one

family. The hole in the bottom could have been made to allow the excess whey to continue to drip. So far, the material has defied identification.

Cherokee Indians

The Cherokees in Tennessee and North Carolina, as well as those in Oklahoma, are well known for their excellent baskets and basketry items. Since they all started in the East and were taught basketry from childhood, there is little difference in the way they make baskets. Probably the biggest difference is that the Eastern group uses more grapevine whereas the Oklahoma group uses buck bush quite a bit.

The backbone of the Cherokee basket industry was, and still is, their oak-splint and cane baskets—the exquisitely colored baskets tinted with old vegetable dyes. Although new baskets are selling well, there is much more interest in the older ones. In fact, those made in the 1940s are commanding prices of $500 to $1000 each. These are the so-called fancy baskets, not the regular work baskets. Many of the work bas-

Basketry cheese mold. 8¼" dia, 3½" h. $35–$50

Cherokee cane basket. 15" dia, 20" h. $600–$800

Cherokee cane basket. 16" dia, 19" h. $700–$850

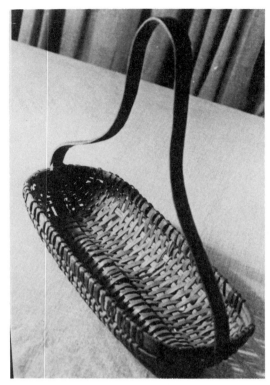

Oak-splint novelty basket, probably Cherokee. $105–$225

Vine basket, probably Oklahoma Cherokees. $150–$250

Oak-splint work basket with colored spokes and weavers. 13" w, 23" l, 18" o.h. $200–$275

kets were made plain, that is, without color, although some were made with bright-colored weavers. All of these baskets have aged over the years to a beautiful patina, and some are almost as desirable today as the fancy or brightly colored baskets.

Unless the history is known, sometimes it is very difficult to ascertain whether an old basket, either work or fancy, was made by Indians or whites. This is especially true of the work baskets, since the Cherokees were a peaceful farming tribe who made and used baskets long before the white man arrived. The white settlers had also been making baskets in their native countries, and brought their skills with them.

The Indians and settlers probably exchanged basketmaking ideas. No doubt they incorporated the best of both methods into the baskets they have continued to make for centuries.

Chestnut Basket

This is not an American-made basket, yet chestnut baskets are showing up in American antique shops, shows, and malls. They were, and maybe still are, being used to ship chestnuts from Portugal—presumably to America, which would explain them being here. They are well-built with spokes as thick as one-half inch, and weavers over one-fourth of an inch thick. That makes a very heavy basket, and one that looks old. The empty basket weighs nine pounds, or about three times as much as a splint basket the same size. Several different sizes have been seen.

Chestnut-shipping basket. 15" w, 18" l, 21" h.
$75–$125

Chinese Basketry, Recent

One of the first trade items offered to Americans after President Nixon opened trade with China was baskets. Wholesalers quickly bought up large stocks and offered them to

Largest of the nested set. 6" w, 7½" l, 3½" h.
$15–$20

the public. Almost everyone bought at least one example.

As far as is known the only type of basket being offered at that time was the nest of four small baskets in natural color only. Later, colored baskets became available. The baskets were well made; in fact, the workmanship was excellent. Originally they came with a red paper label with "The Republic of the People of China" printed in both English and Chinese. These baskets are often seen now in antique shops, malls, and shows, but always singles, never the nested set.

Chinese Wedding Baskets

Chinese wedding baskets have been made for many years, and quite often, older examples will be found in the States. New ones are easily found as they are imported on a regular basis. New Chinese-made baskets can be found every place from specialty stores to discount houses. The newer baskets are a bit drab compared to the older ones with the gaily painted floral designs. They're made in a variety of sizes from 14 to 40 inches. The original use is elusive, but it's safe to assume that brides used them to take special things to their new homes. These baskets, with their three compartments, are useful today for holding anything from mail to sewing projects.

New three-tiered wedding basket with bamboo trim. 9" sq, 15" o.h. $29–$45. Old wedding basket with missing top. Painted design around sides and bamboo trim. 5" w, 9" l, 15" o.h. Damaged, $8–$15; good condition, $28–$45.

Porcupine-quill decorated Chippewa-made box. 3" dia, 2" h. $85–$165

Chippewa Indians

Ojibwas, the original name for this tribe, was corrupted to Chippewa by some of the very first settlers, and in the ensuing years they became better known by that name rather than the original name.

Chippewa Indians lived too far north—from Maine to the Maritimes, through the Great Lakes area of Michigan and Wisconsin, and on into Minnesota, Canada, and parts of Alaska—to depend on agriculture

Birch-bark box with porcupine-quill decoration. Unity College collection. $90–$150

as did so many other tribes. One of the reasons they became scattered over such a large area was their continuous search for better hunting and fishing grounds and for areas with an abundance of birch trees. Birch grows best in those areas, and it was essential to the making of not only their basketry items but also other things such as canoes, containers for fish and game, and buckets for water. It was also needed to make the exquisite porcupine quill work for which they are justifiably proud. The Chippewas still do some porcupine quill work today, and they still use familiar things for designs.

Chitimacha Indians

Baskets were made in North America long before the white man came, but nowhere did it become such a fine art as among the Chitimachas. Throughout their long history they have been noted for their finely crafted and beautifully made baskets. There is only one Chitimacha basketmaker still working, but chances of getting one of her new baskets is rather slim as she is two years behind on orders.

Pride in their heritage, which is exemplified in their basketry, along with the growing demand for their baskets, has caused

Beautifully designed, three-color Chitimacha basket. $1000–$1200

Covered Chitimacha basket. $1300–$1500

Another style Chitimacha basket. $950–$1100

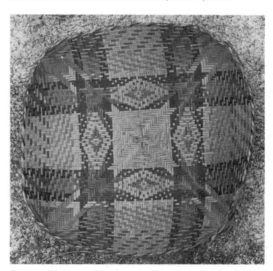

Large Chitimacha three-color tray. $700–$800

at least one of the older Chitimacha basketmakers to talk of returning to basketmaking.

Chitimacha basketmaking is an art form that requires a great deal of skill. In fact, their baskets are not just baskets—they are objects of art, especially the double-woven baskets. *Double-woven* refers to a process that produces two baskets, one inside the other, with a perfect side both inside and out. The double-woven parts share a single rim, and there is no visible place showing where the basket was started and stopped. Double weaving makes a strong, durable basket, and it can be watertight.

Although some rare examples of the old double weave can still be found, they're extremely scarce. On a trip through Louisiana and the Chitimacha reservation, we were unable to find one of their baskets offered

51

for sale. Finally, we were able to photograph some in a private collection.

For generations, the art of basketry was passed down from mother to daughter, but eventually the younger children lost interest—it is a slow, time-consuming chore that doesn't pay that well.

Today, the one remaining Chitimacha basketmaker is selling her large double-woven baskets for as much as $2000, but that is not a spectacular hourly rate when you consider it takes her approximately a month of 8- to 15-hour days to weave the basket. This doesn't include the time spent gathering the cane, or *piya,* as the Chitimachas call it, and the time spent preparing it.

Gathering the piya from the canebrakes along the bayous is a hot, sticky chore. There, the basketmaker selects the tallest and straightest stalks of the bamboo-like cane. She also searches for stalks with the longest joints, because too many joints have a way of disfiguring baskets. The cane, dozens and dozens of stalks, must be kept damp until it is time to split it. When the weaver gets down to the task of splitting the swamp cane, each stalk has to be split, and split again, until the strips are barely a half-inch wide. The smooth outside layer cane is peeled away from the pithy center with the basketmaker's hands and teeth. This leaves the inner white layer, which is placed in the dew for a couple of weeks until the natural green bleaches out.

According to Faye Stouff, who still lives on the reservation, most of the basketmakers are using commercial dyes, but in the old days, the Chitimachas, like all other basketmakers, used vegetable dyes made from plants and roots growing around the reservation. Gathering the dye materials required time and experience, and the actual dying, although not difficult, was time-consuming. To obtain the black that makes one of the dramatic colors in their baskets, the cane had to be boiled in a solution of black walnuts and walnut leaves for nine days. To obtain red, the Cherokees used bloodroot or puccoon; in Louisiana, the Chitimachas used the root of the dock plant, a plant they

called *la passiance,* for red. To obtain their third dramatic color, yellow, they used *powaac* root.

After the swamp cane was dyed and dried, another layer was peeled off, and then the basketmaker was ready to begin the long chore of weaving the basket—a chore that would keep her working for approximately 100 hours on a medium-sized single-weave basket, or 300 to 400 hours on a large double-weave basket.

The Chitimachas are another tribe who have kept the names of the symbols used in their baskets. Designs copied from earlier baskets have little perch (fish) darting around, along with blackbirds' eyes, snake hearts, and turtles. Although these symbols are still used, their origin has been lost, but it had much to do with the Chitimachas' closeness with nature and their dependence on it.

Not only is the origin of the designs lost in the sea of antiquity, the Chitimachas no longer know why they only use three brilliant colors—red, black, and yellow. These colors fade with age, but not as severely as some others.

Choctaw Indians

The Choctaw Indians in Mississippi consider crafts to be a very old, perhaps the oldest, language. Any craft, they believe, allows the worker to express his or her opinions, dreams, and hopes, and if the work is good, it will last for many years—sometimes several lifetimes.

Oak-splint basketry has long been considered men's work among the Choctaws, while swamp-cane baskets were made by women. (This is not to say that the women don't make splint baskets and vice versa, but the majority of the work seems to be divided.) The reason for the division is probably because oak splints were used to make work baskets, which had to be tough and strong, and cane baskets were fancier and easier to make.

Even the large burden baskets had to be as light as possible because the women also used them. These baskets could be at-

Collection of Choctaw baskets.

Old Choctaw cane egg basket. 10" dia, 13" h. $85–$125

Old Choctaw cane basket. 12" dia, 14" h. $95–$145

tached to a tumpline and worn across the head, and in that way could be carried for miles. In the old days, the Choctaw traders might walk all the way from the middle of Mississippi to New Orleans carrying a basket filled with things to sell or trade—things made or grown by the Indians, such as herbs, nuts, and baskets.

The Choctaws have always made baskets, both oak-splint and cane, and today they continue the tradition begun centuries

New Choctaw cane basket. 10" dia, 13" h. $35–$50

New double-weave cane basket, Choctaw. 12" dia, 13" h. $200–$300

ago. Some of the cane baskets are single-weave, others are double-weave, and, just as always, the Choctaws dye the cane to make designs in the baskets.

Today, the Choctaw reservation is filled with new industry, but the Choctaws continue to make baskets as they always have. Appreciation for their basketry, along with good prices, has had a bearing on this continued basketmaking. Twenty-five years ago, cane baskets were selling for under $5 unless they were very old and unusual; now the going price for new ones is around $50 for a medium-size basket, and as high as $350 for a double-woven one.

Church-Offering Basket

In the past, many churches, especially rural churches, used collection or offering baskets, which were long-handled baskets that could be passed up and down the pews to collect the tithes of the parishioners. Church officials would pass the baskets up and down

Rattan church-offering basket. 10" w, 13½" l, 45" l, including handle. $36–$50

either side of the pews, holding the long-handled baskets in front of each person. Some of the baskets were lined with velvet to soften the noise when change was dropped in them.

Cleats

Another name for the reinforcement strips added to the bottom of baskets. See "Runners."

Clematis

Clematis is fast becoming a cultivated plant, but there was a time when much of it grew wild and was used frequently in basket-making. It is a woody climbing plant of the *crowfoot* family and is very desirable as a garden plant, due to its large, brightly colored blue, pink, purple, and white flowers. Clematis was used both for spokes and weavers, and was sometimes mixed with other vines to make baskets.

Clothes Hamper

Hampers have long been a favorite place to store one's clothing, both clean and dirty. Actually, the first mention of a hamper—or what was later identified as a hamper—was in the will of a man who died in 1675. Among

Factory-made splint hamper. 13" w, 18" l, 27" h. $15–$20

his choice possessions was one "Wikker Flasket."

People have long made woven hampers. The first ones were made of willow, or—as the man described it—"wikker," while others were made of various splints. Most of the early hampers were made by hand, but later, the majority were factory-made. During the past quarter century, woven hampers have suffered a decline in popularity because of built-in storage spaces in modern homes.

Clothespin Baskets

For Clothespins

Beautiful, old, handmade baskets have not always been as treasured as they are now. They were made and used for specific chores. When they were no longer needed for those chores, or had been replaced by boxes and bags, they were discarded or relegated to mundane chores like holding "plunder" or clothespins. This basket is shown just as it

Willow clothes hamper. 18" w, 24" l, 24" h. $35–$50

Clothespin basket with plywood bottom. 12" dia. $5–$15

Well-made oak-splint basket with low handle. 9½" dia, 13" o.h. $125–$195

was taken from a basement to be sold in an estate auction. The owner had been very practical in finding a new use for it, as the basket would have only sold for a few dollars at the time she converted it to a clothespin basket. It probably served her well because it was very sturdy and it moved easily up and down the clothesline. At the auction it sold for $155.

Of Clothespins

This is not a basket *for* clothespins, but rather a basket made *of* clothespins. This intricately fashioned basket was made 40 years ago by a man who used regular spring-type wooden clothespins to make this basket for his small granddaughter.

Coasters

It is doubtful that many basketmakers made coasters for their own use, but they made many styles to sell to the tourists. This is one of the later basketry items, having originated around 1915 to 1920. The Cherokees still make coasters using honeysuckle vine dyed with walnut and bloodroot. Indians in the Southwest also made twined coasters to sell to the tourists.

Honeysuckle vine coaster made by the Cherokees. 5" dia. $3–$7

Double-woven coaster made by the Indians of the Southwest. 3" dia. $25–$40

Cochineal

Cochineal is a scale insect that is a native of the warmer climates of America. It can be found in several species of cactus, especially the Indian fig tree. Red dye for baskets was made from the bodies of the females.

Coiled-Straw Baskets

This type basketry may have originated in Germany, where it is believed to have been first used to make beehives, but it was perfected by the Germans who moved to Pennsylvania. They used the coiled straw to make containers and baskets for their chores. Rye was the first straw used for these baskets, and later the Pennsylvania Germans used whatever straw was available. These baskets are still made by a few of the old bas-

Old coiled-straw basket. 8″ dia, 20″ o.h. $25–$50

ketmakers, and even some of the old baskets can still be found.

Coiling

Unlike the woven basket that has spokes and weavers, the coiled basket is made from one long, flexible rod made of tightly coiled cattails, rush, willow, corn husk, or any of a number of other materials. The rod or coil may be covered completely with raffia, yucca, palm leaves, or other materials, and then sewn together at intervals. Or, it can be sewn together not only to hold it, but to form a design.

Small baskets can be made either by coiling or weaving, but coiling is recommended for tiny ones. Like the woven basket, the coiled one can be made in any shape—round, square, oval, oblong—but it is best suited to a round shape.

Coil Wrap

Some of the people making baskets during the first decades of this century used a method called *coil wrap* in which they used leftover yarn and threads to cover grass (or rush) to make coil basketry items. A few of these can still be found and are usually displayed with other baskets. During the past few years, this method of basketry has been

Coil-wrapped basket. 4″ dia, 4½″ h. $7.50–$12.50

revived, but with a new twist. Now the coils are generally made of large scraps of fabric and are wrapped with other colorful strips of fabric.

Compote, Woven

Compotes woven of various basketry materials are seen occasionally. The workmanship on some is excellent, while others, although made with much fancier designs, still lack skilled workmanship. The illustration is an example of the latter. For one thing, the splints are not top quality, and they are too wide. There are too many decorations—like the curliques and miniature baskets hanging around the sides. The idea would have worked better with smaller splints; nevertheless, it's a beautiful piece of primitive basketry. Some of the weavers

were dyed green, others red, but through the years they have faded almost completely. The miniature woven baskets hanging around the bottom of the bowl measure one inch in diameter, and are two inches in overall height. It was covered with black cobwebs when found, indicating it had been stored for many years.

Copper Basket, Contemporary

Old copper berry baskets are hard to find today, but new ones are being made. Michael Bonne, a coppersmith in Carthage, Indiana, made this one. He uses the old methods and tools to make an assortment of copper wares.

Most basket collections are displayed in rooms with fireplaces, and nothing increases the beauty of the collection like the reflection of the fire in a few copper baskets.

Ash-splint woven compote. 10" dia, 7" h. $35–$60

New copper basket. 6" w, 7" l, 7½" o.h. $20–$25

Finely cut ash-splint compote with wrapped handles and reinforced base. Some splints are dyed green and brown, while others are left natural. 12" dia, 6¼" h. $60–$98

Coralberry

Another name for Indian currant. See "Indian Currant."

Corn Husk Basketry

Corn husk basketry has been called a Southern craft. If it were strictly a Southern craft it would be called corn *shuck* basketry, as shuck is the common Southern name for the outside husk of an ear of corn.

Outside the South, Northern Indians made corn husk masks to be used in planting and harvesting celebrations. They may have also made other basketry items with the corn husks such as hats, fans, mats, and bags, as well as baskets. The husks or shucks were twisted and used to make seats (*bottom-chairs*), hearth brooms, and mops.

In the South, mops were made by boring holes in a small oblong piece of wood and attaching a handle. The corn husks were twisted and then pulled through the holes leaving over half the husks to form the mop.

Corn husks could be used in a number of ways to make basketry items. They could be braided and the braids sewn together in circles or squares to make mats. They could also be folded into small pointed pieces and sewn on cardboard or buckram to make hats. Although it was seldom done, they could be woven on the old looms to make table mats or place mats, or used as the base for coiled basketry. Sometimes they were rolled into a hard core, wrapped with raffia, and used to make coiled Indian baskets (described in various instruction books on basketry published around the turn of the century).

Cornmeal Sieve and Tray

Corn might have been one of the most plentiful foods for both the Indian and white families, and corn bread can be very tasty, but even corn bread lovers admit it is not very good when it is filled with husks and hulls. The Indian women learned how to grind the corn in mortars, made from hollowed-out stones and logs, with pestles also made of stone or with maul-type wooden pestles. They tried winnowing the corn, but soon decided a sieve fashioned after the hominy sieve but with smaller openings would work better. The ground meal was sifted through the sieve leaving the husk behind. The meal was caught in the tray.

The need for cornmeal sieves and trays disappeared long ago, which accounts for their scarcity today. One can be found for sale occasionally, and they can be seen in some Indian museums. In the early days

Ladies' corn husk hat. $75–$100

Swamp-cane cornmeal sieve and tray. Sieve, $8\frac{1}{2}$" sq, 2" h; tray, $10\frac{1}{2}$" sq, $2\frac{1}{2}$" h. $79–$105 for set.

they were probably made of many different kinds of material, but most seen today are made of cane.

Corn-Shaped Basketry

During the heyday of basketry souvenir making, the Passamaquoddies began making baskets that resembled various foods. No doubt others joined in, but credit for the beginning of this type of basketry is given to the Passamaquoddy tribe.

One of the most attractive "food baskets" is the one shaped like an ear of corn. It's very realistic and even has silks. It's woven of tough, but flexible, paper-thin ash splints with circles to represent the individual grains. The top has a sweet-grass handle, a sort of trademark of the Passamaquoddy-made food baskets. Pumpkin baskets were dyed orange and acorn baskets were dyed green, but if the corn basket was dyed yellow, the color has faded. It is the natural golden color of ash.

Corn-Sifting Basket

Some people prefer this name to cornmeal sieve or tray. See "Corn Meal Sieve and Tray."

Corn-Washing Basket

The Senecas, who are famous for the corn-washing basket, used twill weaving to make the baskets for the added strength that that type of weaving provides. The basket was designed and used to rinse dried corn kernels that had been cooked in hot ashes. The cooking turned the corn into hominy, and when it was done, the ashes and hulls had to be washed or rinsed away. The bottoms of the baskets are done in an open, checkered weave that allows the water to flow out freely, taking the ashes and hulls with it. The Senecas are still making corn-washing baskets along with other basketry items they have made through the years.

New, Seneca-made ash-splint corn-washing basket. 12" sq, 10" h. New, $25–$35; old, $75–$125.

Cotton Basket

Shortly after the settlers arrived in the southern states they began to grow cotton. Until mills were built in the North, the cot-

Ash and sweet-grass basket shaped like an ear of corn. Unity College collection. $50–$75

Oak-splint cotton basket. 18" dia, 19" h. $65–$95

ton was shipped to England to be made into fabric. There was a problem with seed removal, but Eli Whitney solved that one with his gin. This really paved the way for the growth of cotton.

To harvest the fields of cotton the pickers had to go in with long osnaburg cotton sacks they filled by picking the fluffy white bolls—one at a time. Rather than let the pickers lose valuable time walking long distances to a waiting wagon or to the barn, the grower made or bought numerous oak-splint cotton baskets that were placed at either end of the row, sometimes in the middle of long rows. Each picker or family of pickers had a basket.

The baskets of cotton were weighed at night, and then the pickers were paid for their labors. Cotton baskets of approximately the same size were never weighed separately, as it was an accepted fact that large cotton baskets weighed 8 pounds; therefore, 8 pounds was automatically deducted from the total of each basket of cotton.

Unfortunately, the days of the cotton basket were numbered. Shortly after the turn of the present century, the basket began to be replaced by cotton spreads, large squares of osnaburg. It was much easier to empty cotton sacks on the spreads, as they didn't have to pack the cotton in as they did in the baskets, and the spreads were easy to move and store. By this time, cotton was no longer king in the South, as farming was becoming more diversified, and the demise of the cotton basket didn't seem to matter. In a few years it would all be replaced by the mechanical cotton picker.

But the old cotton baskets continued to be used around the farm for a few chores—like harvesting corn, potatoes, and cabbages. A few of the old baskets have survived. These baskets are not as popular as other types. Today they're used for wood for the fireplace or for magazines.

Cottonwood

One of several trees of the genus *Populus,* cottonwood grows mostly in the eastern part of the country and is called cottonwood because the flowers have scaly spikes, no petals, and cottonlike tufts on the seeds. The flower closely resembles those on the willow and birch, and like the willow the shoots can be used in basketry. They are tough and flexible which makes them perfect for either spokes or weavers. The shoots or rods may be split several times to make fine splints for weaving. Flexible cottonwood shoots have also been used as the foundation for coiled baskets, and it is said that many Indian gambling baskets had cottonwood foundations.

Coushatta Indians

The Coushatta tribe was well established in America when DeSoto arrived. Records show DeSoto and his men kidnapped the chief and some of the tribe leaders but released them shortly thereafter. Following that brief and terrifying experience, the Coushattas began a peaceful coexistence with the white man that lasted through most of the seventeenth century. Then in 1783, treaties were broken and wars broke out in which thousands of warriors were lost, and the

New pine needle basket with Indian head on top. 4" dia, 6" h. $20–$25

Another style new pine needle basket. 10" dia, 11¼" o.h. $25–$30

New pine needle basket with open-work design. 9" dia, 12" o.h. $23–$46

Coushattas had to give up millions of acres of their land.

It became apparent they would have to search for a place where they could live in peace. Late in the eighteenth century, one of the Coushatta leaders, Red Shoes (who was known as King of the Alabamas and Coushattas), lead a band of 80 to 100 men to the banks of the Red River in Louisiana. Several other moves followed, and by 1884, most of the Coushattas had settled near Elton, Louisiana, in Allen Parish, where they remain today.

The Coushattas have always made exquisite baskets and basketry items. A historical marker standing on the highway that leads to the reservation says the following: "Coushatta Indians, three miles north, is a tribe that migrated in 1795 to Louisiana from Alabama. Name means 'white reed brake'; Coushatta town in Red River parish named for them. Noted for basket handicraft." Indeed, they are noted for their fine baskets and have justified their name Coushatta or "white reed brake." (Originally, the Coushattas were known as Koastis.)

Some Coushattas still make the swampcane or reed baskets, but today they are best known for their coiled pine needle baskets. Not only do they make baskets using pine needles, but they also make effigies of the animals they are familiar with, the ones that live near them. Both men and women make baskets. They wrap the pine needles in colored raffia to make crawfish, ducks, chickens, armadillos, owls, and turtles. They also make a small covered pine needle box or basket with an Indian head on top. Black raffia makes the hair, while small black stitches form the eyes. Red forms the lips.

Covered Baskets

Covers and lids were made for all kinds of baskets, depending on the basket's use as well as the whim of the maker. In most areas, in the early days, baskets had covers to keep out the mice, rats, and squirrels. That also explains why so many of the storage-type baskets were made of thicker splints—it was more difficult for the rodents to chew through them. Sewing baskets, sewing stands, pie baskets, lunch baskets, and picnic baskets usually had covers or lids.

Small pine needle covered box (new) made by 80-year-old man. 3" dia, 2" h. $10–$15

New vase and covered box made of pine needles. $15–$25

Plain ash-splint pie basket. 11" dia, 5" h. $30–$50

Covered ash-splint basket. Unity College collection. $45–$75

Three ash-splint baskets: (bottom) 14" dia, 10" h,
$44–$68; *(middle) 12" dia, 10" h,* ***$50–$74;*** *(top)*
6" dia, 3½" h, ***$18–$33.***

Covered ash-splint basket. 8" dia, 4" h. ***$35–$65***

Covers

See "Lids and Covers."

Cradles

Baby

Willow baby cradles have been used in America since the Pilgrims landed. There was usually a new baby in the family every year, so the cradles were in constant use.

Like the wooden baby-tender, the cradle was an absolute necessity. The mother had to go about her chores, and with the cradle she didn't have to hold the child. She could leave it in the cradle and rock it as she passed by.

In time other types of cradles would be made, but none was ever as popular as the

Old wicker doll cradle. 10" w, 20" l, 10" h. ***$95–$125***

Willow cradle approximately 200 years old with only a little damage at the base of the hood on the right side. ***$500–$1200***

willow (unless it was the hooded, wooden cradle). Parents seldom, if ever, took the cradle with them when going to church or socials. Instead, they used a large basket. No doubt it was easier to handle than a cradle.

Old willow cradles are extremely difficult to find today, which means prices are high for those in good-to-excellent condition.

Doll

About a century ago one of the few jobs most girls could look forward to was that of homemaker. Knowing that, parents trained them well. Girls often played with dolls and in playhouses. This accounts for the large number of *housekeeping toys* like doll cradles. These doll cradles were made of oak and ash splint, and of willow. During the

1920s, a cheaper version of the wicker was made—today, it is quite collectible.

Miniature

Since people first learned to weave willow, grasses, splints, and other materials into useful items, they have made cradles—sometimes for the baby, other times for the children's dolls, and oftentimes just to test their skills and ability.

Most of the small ash-splint cradles were made by four Indian tribes, the Penobscots, the Passamaquoddies, the Maliseets, and the Micmacs. Each of these groups made cradles to be sold to tourists, the visitors com-

This tiny oak-splint piece is called a miniature cradle by the owner. $135–$150

Ash-splint doll cradle probably made by the Passamaquoddy Indians. 8" w, 16" l, 13" h. $99–$150

Late wicker doll cradle. $35–$55

Old ash-splint hooded miniature cradle. Unity College collection. $60–$95

Ash-splint miniature cradle (left), 7½" l, 6" h. $50–$85 Late cradle, rockers missing. 6" l, 5½" h. $20–$30

Creel with leather trim. $150–$175

ing into Maine during the summers a century or so ago. Today, these miniatures are avidly sought by both miniature and novelty collectors.

Vine as well as fine oak-splint examples are known, and the latter is believed to have been made by both the Cherokees and the settlers in the Great Smoky and Ozark mountains.

Creel

A *creel* is a woven basket used to hold a fisherman's catch until he or she is ready to go home. Some are primitively made, while others are elaborate. They're all odd-shaped little baskets—some plain, and others with genuine leather trim.

A decade ago there was little demand for used creels; thus, you could buy one for less than $5. But there is much more demand now, and it's not unusual to see a

Crudely made ash-splint creel. 7" w, 11" l, 12½" h. $28–$45

dozen or more creels displayed in one booth at the larger antique shows. They're usually used for decorative purposes, either to hang on the wall or place on a desk or table. With the prices of ordinary fishing creels skyrocketing, it is no longer advisable to paint the plain ones and use them for plant holders (although they do make attractive ones!).

Creel used as plant holder. $55–$115

Crocheted Basket

Needleworkers have always crocheted some baskets, but the current popularity of baskets in general has caused many more to be made recently. This is a good example of how baskets can be made of any material, using a variety of methods.

Crocheted basket. 2" dia, 2½" o.h. $5

Large crocheted basket. Heavily starched to hold its shape. 6" w, 9½" l, 9" h. $15–$20

Crooked Knife

It is believed that all Indian basketmakers in the Northeast, as well as most of the white ones, made and used crooked knives for the making of their baskets. The blade comes out of the handle at a crooked angle, hence the name. The handle is also crooked, but this is done to compensate for the position in which the knife is usually held so that it works more efficiently and is more comfortable to use. More than anything else, the crooked knife is used to make the points or pointy look on rims and handles.

One of the reasons for attributing some of the crooked knives to the white basketmakers are the initials carved on many of them. It isn't that likely the Indians would have used three English letters. Talking to various basketmakers it has been found that

Crooked knife with handmade blade and missing rim. Fancy carved design on end; initials "W.C.S." 11" l. $30–$55

each person preferred, if possible, to make his or her own knife so it would fit the individual's own hands and needs.

Cutters for Ash Splint

Makers of ash-splint baskets had to be inventive. They not only had to devise a comb to be used on the sweet grass, but they also had to make cutters and knives to split the ash strips into assorted sizes. They made a wooden handle onto which they attached sharpened springs or wires from a clock; some used strong piano wires. The cutters were grasped by the handle and slowly and smoothly pulled along the length of a strip of ash. Depending on the cutter used, the pull would produce anything from a very fine to a half-inch wide strip; the cutters could cut from 6 to 12 strips at one time.

Five assorted cutters for ash splint. Note the carved design on the handle in the middle. $50–$65 each

Decorating a New Basket

To add a personal and decorative touch to a new basket that is to be given to a child or taken to a shut-in, weave brightly colored ribbon or fabric into it. On this basket the plaid fabric was cut into strips twice the width needed, then folded over to make a "right" side both inside and out. It was run through the basket and glued together under the handle on the inside.

Factory-made basket with plaid fabric weavers. 5″ dia, 8″ o.h. $5–$8

Decorating with Baskets

Baskets lend themselves to nearly any arrangement, whether it is composed of simple greenery, cut or dried flowers, vegetables, or nuts. Arrangements are a great way to used damaged or new baskets. The damage can either be covered by the arrangement, or it can be turned to the back where it won't show. Some baskets can be painted before they are used to make them more attractive. Perhaps the most attractive thing about using baskets as containers for arrangements is the fact that they can be changed as often as desired. For instance, the half basket in the photograph was painted white to cover a big, black stain in the bottom. It is used in the fall to hold autumn leaves, and then at Christmas it is filled with holly and candy canes are hung around the rim. In summer it is used to hold cut flowers after a metal container is placed inside to hold water.

Blooming potted plants can also be used in baskets and are very attractive, but the basket should be lined with aluminum foil or some other material that will stop water from seeping through to the basket.

White half basket with berry and leaves arrangement.

New, cheap basket filled with artificial eggs and berries.

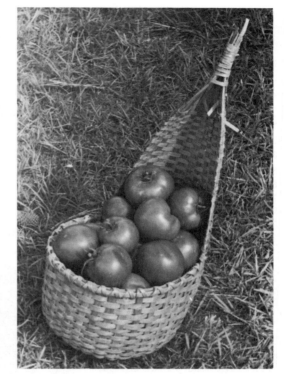

Basket filled with tomatoes fits nicely in the kitchen.

Dried arrangement in hand basket. $100–$150

Dried arrangement in swing-handle basket. $250–$400

Devil's Claw

Devil's claw or *devil's horn* are the common names for the herbaceous plant *Martynia,* named for the Cambridge University botanist John Martyn (1699–1768). The plant has clammy-smelling leaves, large violet blossoms, and dark green pods.

The pods are the only part of the plant used. They are gathered and split into fine strips to add color to baskets. Several tribes use devil's claw in their basketry, but the Papagos use it most often. Since the color of the dried pods can vary from dark gray to black, they're usually dyed to get an even color. The dyed devil's claw is then bound in with yucca to cover the willow or bear grass foundation. Using devil's claw involves much work; therefore, baskets with this decoration are higher priced, sometimes twice as much as plain yucca baskets.

Devil's Horn

Another name for the herbaceous plant *Martynia.* See "Devil's Claw".

Dish Drainer Basket

This basket is large enough to hold dishes and may or may not have been used as a dish drainer. It's made of an unknown, pithy-type vine. The larger-sized vines were used for the spokes or standards and the braided border, while smaller ones were used for weavers.

Vine dish-drainer basket. 13½" dia, 5" h. $35–$50

Doll's Fan

During those souvenir-making days, the basketmakers left nothing to chance—if they thought something would sell, they made it. The small doll fan is a case in point. It was a wonderful 5-cent gift for a child who would enjoy it because she could fan her doll just like the mothers fanned their babies.

Doll fan made of ash splint and sweet grass. 2½" dia, 5" h (including the handle). $7–$10

Doll's Furniture

In 1959 an English basketmaker published a book of instructions for making various types of basketry items. Two of those items were a chair and sofa (like the ones in the photograph) made for a small doll. The maker of this rattan set changed the style of the chair making it a tub-type; the original instructions were for a chair exactly like the sofa. Also, a round rattan table was added.

Miniature sofa $3\frac{1}{2}$" w, $7\frac{1}{2}$" l, 4" h; chair 3" w, 4" l, 4" h; table 5" dia, $3\frac{1}{4}$" h. $35–$50

It is possible that two sets were mixed and the tub-type chair just ended up with this sofa.

Among the instructions for other unusual smalls were ones for a baby rattle and the following miniatures: cane rattle, fruit bowl, cradle, shopping basket, and carpet beater.

Double-Woven Baskets

Many of the early baskets were double woven so they could be waterproofed. Then, as water containers came into use, the need for waterproof baskets decreased. Several tribes, especially the Cherokee and Choctaw, made some double-woven baskets for their own use and for sale.

As basket collecting grows in popularity, basketmakers are quickly reverting to the craft of double woven baskets. They are made of swamp or river cane and are dyed in several colors.

Double-Wrapped Rim

To make a double-wrap or X-binding on the top or the rim of splint baskets, the weaver wrapped the top in one direction, then reversed the procedure for the second time around. When completed, the top of the basket was covered with a double row of binding making it very strong and sturdy. Collectors usually prefer double-wrapped rims.

Double-woven Choctaw with different design. 12" dia, 14" h. $200–$300

Double-woven Choctaw basket. 10" dia, 13" h. $200–$300

71

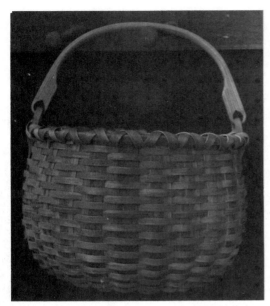

Basket with double-wrapped rim. $400–$600

Dowel Basket

Before the appearance of the machine-made brown paper bag in 1883, customers had no choice other than to take their purchases home in small shopping bags or have them delivered by the store, if it were a larger market.

Paper bags had existed prior to that time, but they weren't plentiful due to the fact they had to be glued together by hand, which naturally made them very expensive. Our "waste not, want not" ancestors weren't about to pay good money for bags that were destructible when they had durable splint and willow baskets. So it wasn't until 1883, when Charles Stilwell invented a machine to make bags, that baskets even started to be replaced—and then it took a long, long time.

One of the reasons it took people so long to adjust to paper bags was habit. Another was the fact they didn't buy everything as we do now. They raised most of their produce and had milk, butter, eggs, and some produce delivered by farmers.

It has been reported that Americans use 40 billion paper bags annually now, and that

Factory-made dowel basket. 16" w, 27" l, 11" h. $45–$65

figure is probably correct as the average wife today brings home from five to ten bags of groceries per week whereas the turn-of-the-century housewife brought all her purchases home in her shopping basket, or they were delivered to her in a basket similar to the dowel basket.

The dowel basket was made by a factory set up to make this type basket, as evidenced by the fact that the dowels are all cut to fit. The tops are rounded and the bottoms shaped to fit in with other shaped dowels that form the base. This basket was commonly used to deliver groceries and later was relegated to use as a laundry basket.

Drags

Drags is a very descriptive name used for the reinforcement strips added on the bottom of baskets to allow them to be dragged when they are too heavy to carry. Drags also protected the bottom when the weight was excessive. See "Runners."

Drawing Horse

Same as shaving horse. See "Shaving Horse."

Draw Knife

A tool with a very sharp blade with two handles. A sort of miniature two-man saw with a smooth blade, it is used for making splints and for cutting and smoothing off the rough places.

Dress Hats, Caps

The finely woven hats and caps made and worn by both Indian men and women could more rightly be described as skull caps of a sort.

Most Indians wore hats at one time or another, some to protect themselves from rain and sun, others to alleviate some of the pressure from the tumpline. The *tumpline* was a head strap that was attached to a burden basket. The basket was hung on the back and the tumpline placed across the head.

The hats and caps served as a kind of protection.

The Hupas made lovely woven hats and caps, as did other tribes, including the Karoks and the Yuroks. The Utes also made hats, but of a coarser texture. The Haidas made a hat with a flaring brim. These hats and caps are often mistaken for bowls.

Dryer, Woven

This woven, handmade dryer may have been used to dry apples, but not unless the apples were cut into large pieces. It could have been used to dry other things or other fruits. Beans were usually strung to dry, but it's possible someone decided to try this method.

Finely woven hat, probably made by the Hupas. $250–$450

Woven dryer with dowel-type frame. 16" by 19" w, 2½" h. $56–$85

Finely woven old Hupa hat. 7" dia, 3" h. $300–$500

Durability of Baskets

The life of a basket depends on several factors. Probably the most important factor is workmanship, with materials and use following closely. Care of baskets also has some bearing on their survival. It is a good idea

Two willow baskets approximately 150 years old.

to put baskets out in the rain at least once a year, if not twice.

The exact age of the two willow baskets shown in the photograph is not known, but they were being used on a seagoing ship that wrecked off the coast of Maine in 1848. They washed ashore and were picked up by people living nearby. They are still in excellent condition, except for a few weavers that were probably torn apart when the baskets were dashed against the rocks before they were picked up.

Dyes

Blue

See "Indigo."

Brown

Brown dye could be made from several things, but walnut bark was the favorite for making dark brown dye. The bark could also be used for making black dye by using additional ingredients and a longer boiling time.

A light, soft brown dye was made from the bark of butternut.

Green

Very little green dye was used on baskets because it was so difficult to make. No green dye has been seen on old baskets from the South and Midwest; however, it was used sparingly in the Northeast and probably in Canada. It could be made, if one had the patience, by boiling together white cedar twigs and elm bark for quite some time. The dye had to be set with coperas, and after all the time-consuming, tedious work, it seldom turned out to be a true green, but rather a yellow-green. Probably the only advantage of using green dye was that it seldom, if ever, faded.

Red

One of the favorite red dyes of the early settlers, the Cherokee Indians of the Great Smoky mountains, and the Ozarks was made with *cochineal* (a dye made from the bodies of insects). In New England, much of the red dye was made from berries. One of New England's favorite berries came from a plant called *Solomon's seal* (often called *Nahurmominin* or *eel berries*).

Like the mountaineers and Cherokees, New England makers also used bloodroot to obtain red dye. Another plant of the same family, called *puccoon,* was used to make an orangey red. Blueberries were used to obtain a reddish pink, but that particular dye didn't have the lasting power of some of the other reds—it faded more quickly. Various solutions had to be used to "set" the colors.

Yellow

Yellow dye could be made from several materials, including woodchips from the *fustic* tree. Some basketmakers used yellow root or sumac, depending on what was available in the area. In the Northeast, they used the roots of *goldthread* (*Coptis trifolia*), an evergreen plant whose yellow roots were also used in medicine. The dye made from goldthread was strong, clear, brilliant, and long-lasting. In Louisiana and other parts of the South, basketmakers used a plant called

74

butterweed, which grows wild, to make yellow dye.

Earring Baskets

Shortly after people began to travel extensively and spend summers at spas, basketmakers began making souvenirs to sell to those tourists. In an effort to increase sales, basketmakers made every conceivable type of basketry souvenir. One of those souvenirs was earrings.

Beginning around 1920 they made a tiny basket that could be attached to clip-on earrings. Recently the clip-ons have given way to fasteners for pierced ears. They continued to be popular well into the 1940s. Made of finely cut ash splints and sweet grass, the little baskets are not as durable as they might have been, especially when they were discarded after the novelty had worn off.

The popularity of baskets and basketry during the past decade or so has probably surpassed its previous record. This has enticed retired basketmakers to return to work, and they are reviving some of the old souvenirs. It is even possible now to find a few pairs of basket earrings.

New basket earrings. ⅜" dia, 1" o.h. $12–$20

Easter Baskets

Compared to Easter eggs and Easter rabbits, the Easter basket is a late bloomer. It has only been within the last century that candy eggs became accepted for use at Easter, and the basket became accepted about the same time.

When the Easter basket first became popular, people who could make baskets made them for their children; others bought them from a neighborhood basketmaker. The baskets might be made of anything from splints to pine needles—whatever material was available.

Realizing the popularity of the Easter baskets, merchants began importing them from the Orient—and parents began buying them. The larger baskets were designed to

Two small rice-paper Easter baskets. 3" dia, 3" h. $5–$8

Handmade Easter basket of the type very popular in the 1920s. Splint and rattan with vine handle. 8" w, 11" l, 16" o.h. $25–$30

hold a rabbit, several boiled and colored eggs, a bag of candy eggs, and maybe a small gift. Small rice-paper baskets made in China were included in the nest where the Easter bunny had "laid" the large basket. The small ones were essential for children who insisted on taking their Easter basket to church on Sunday. The small ones were much easier to manage, and the child was usually satisfied.

Eel Traps

Both Indians and Pilgrims enjoyed eating eels, and they shared practical ways of catching them. One of the most primitive methods was treading the eels out of brooks and streams using bare feet and then catching them with bare hands.

They also made eel traps, which were necessary in order to catch a large number of eels. The Indians were quite skilled at this form of basketry—they had had more experience than the Pilgrims with the materials in the area.

Like all handmade items, the traps were made to fit the needs of the user. Small traps were used in shallow streams, while the large ones were used in the ocean. Regardless of where they were used, the design of the traps was the same—a more or less cone-shaped apparatus with one or two cone-shaped inserts inside.

The large traps were anchored on the ocean floor with a buoy to identify the spot, and bait was placed inside the trap to attract the eels. Once inside, the eel was unable to get out as the top of the trap was covered with some sort of bag or stopper. When a fisherman pulled up the trap, he simply uncovered the top, allowing the eels to swim out and into his boat.

The eel trap shown in the illustration was made by the Wampanoag Indians. This one is made of cedar roots because it was believed to be the longest lasting material for traps.

Cedar-root eel trap made by Wampanoags. 6" dia top, 19" dia bottom, 6' 9" h. $195–$260

76

Bottom of eel trap showing first insert.

Egg Basket

A variety of styles and types of egg baskets were used in different places. Throughout most of the Midwest, the Ozarks, the Appalachians, and some of the border states, the *gizzard* or *buttocks* basket was known as the *egg basket*. Further south, both the whites and the blacks made square and round oak-splint baskets for eggs. The southern Indians, especially the Choctaws, made a pretty, round cane egg basket. In the Northeast, there wasn't a special basket just for eggs.

But baskets of one kind or another were used universally, if not for gathering and taking the eggs to the store, then for storing them in the home. There were also smaller baskets that resembled the hen basket that was used in parts of Kentucky and Tennessee. The basket's flat sides fit well against the horse's neck when one had to take the eggs to the store on horseback.

Choctaw cane egg basket. 10" dia, 13" h. $115–$175

Small eel trap found hanging from rafters of old house. 35" h, 10" dia. $67–$95

Small basket similar to those used in the mountains to take eggs on horseback. **$40–$65**

Buttocks or gizzard egg basket. 10" dia, 12" h. **$200–$325**

Square oak-splint Deep South egg basket. 8" sq, 13" o.h. **$110–$150**

In some areas, these baskets were used for gathering and storing eggs, especially large duck, geese, and turkey eggs. Notice the crudely carved duck decoy in front. Left, **$30–$46;** *right,* **$50–$75.**

Elbow Basket

Originally, the elbow basket was made to keep valuables. It was carried on the arm like a purse and hung on a wall when not in use.

But, as most basketmakers and collectors know, baskets are used for a multitude of purposes, often not the purposes for which the baskets were made, as was the case of the elbow basket, shown here. This finely split cane basket was photographed in the home of a Chitimacha basketmaker, who said she made it especially for her son when he was a young boy. It was used as a place to keep his toothbrush and toothpaste.

Chitimacha-made cane elbow basket, 16" w, 14" l. $400–$500

Elm

Both elm splints and elm roots have been used in basketry. Makers used whatever was most suitable and most plentiful in the area. Elm trees seem to be more plentiful in Wisconsin and the surrounding areas. For that reason the Winnebagos and Chippewas seem to have used more elm in their basketry.

Embroidered Baskets

Several craft people have been successful with cross-stitched (embroidered) designs on the new loosely woven basketry items such as flat bowls, mats, trays, and fans. The weaving has to be even for best results. The smaller, more tightly woven pieces can be used as long as there is enough space between the spokes and weavers for the thread. Either fewer strands or smaller thread must be used on these baskets. Rug and left-over sweater yarns can be used on the looser-woven baskets.

There are numerous new bamboo items for sale in gift and discount stores. These can be converted from mundane pieces to one-of-a-kind basketry items by cross-stitching designs on them much like those stitched on fabric.

English Ivy

English ivy either grows wild or can be cultivated. In basketmaking, the larger vines are used for spokes and the smaller ones for weavers.

Eskimo Baskets

The word *Eskimo* was coined back in 1611 by a Jesuit. He had heard the Alaskan people referred to as *eskimantsik* by the neighboring Indians, and he translated that to Eskimo. At the time, the Eskimos called themselves *Inuit*, which is plural of *inuk* (man).

Even then, the Eskimos were making baskets. They had no other containers, so baskets were essential. With their many years of experience, it's only natural they would make excellent baskets, and they have another advantage over other basketmakers—their winters are so long they can make plenty of them.

Yupik Eskimo basket, seal-gut decoration. 8" h, 5" dia. $140–$190

For their best baskets, the Eskimos go out on the tundra and along the shores of Alaska's Bering Sea where they gather a type of rough, but pliable, beach grass. During the late summer, the grasses are carefully selected, and then bleached and cured. The grass will be used during the long winter.

They also gather tundra and rye grass that covers the southwestern coast of Alaska to make the Yupik coiled baskets. The foundation for the coils is usually made from a bundle of grass; then, the stitches spiral around the foundation with each stitch interlocking the coil beneath it. At one time, the Eskimos decorated their baskets with animal parts, feathers, beads, and other objects. Now, their decorations consist mostly of sewing in dyed grass or laying seal gut over the already-sewn stitches. Before, colors were obtained from alder bark and berries, and willow, but like basketmakers all over the country, they too are beginning to use commercial dyes.

Most still use specific shapes, designs, and styles that are characteristic of particular Eskimo villages. One of the best known is the small, Hooper Bay–shaped ginger jar.

Eskimo basket with tall handles. Seal-gut decoration. 7" w, 15" l, 5" h. $135–$197

Factory-Made Baskets

Contrary to popular belief, factory-made baskets are almost completely "handmade"—the 46 individual hand operations are carried out by individuals on an assembly-type operation.

Sidney Gage and Company—better known as Basketville—in Putney, Vermont, describes the factory there as "the largest manufacturer of handmade baskets in the United States." They are said to produce the best baskets that can be made using assembly-line manufacturing. The same family has owned the factory since 1842 with the fourth generation now in charge. Some

Older factory-made picnic basket. 8" w, 13" l, 15" o.h. $23–$40

Smaller, solid-top picnic basket. 6" w, 10" l, 11" o.h. $25–$46

80

Older double-handled laundry basket, factory-made. 18" w, 24" l, 17" o.h. $25–$40

Small, round, decorated factory-made basket. 4" dia, 8" h. $14–$23

Old, small factory-made basket. $19–$31

of their earlier baskets have already reached antique status.

Making baskets under factory conditions is not much different from making them at home—only the operation is larger, with as many labor-saving devices as possible.

They begin with the same knot-free ash and oak splints that have been cut to size. Just as the individual basketmaker must soften the wood before cutting the splints, so does the factory. The factory must do it quickly, as workers may be waiting on materials; therefore, the wood is softened in vats of hot water. The splints are cut by hand with draw knives much like those used by individuals. The difference in the factory is that there may be a half dozen workers cutting splints at any one time. The splints are then treated with steam or hot water to make them pliable enough to fit the basket forms, and again, large amounts are treated at one time as there are many workers using them.

Decorated, factory-made, half-bushel apple basket. $65–$80

When the splints are ready, they're given to the worker who will weave the bottom of the basket. The bottoms are woven rapidly and placed in a rack for the weavers, who will shape and weave them over the forms or molds.

The baskets are then sent by conveyor to workers who will fasten bands around the top and attach handles. Lids may be attached to those requiring them. Some lids are painted and decorated before being attached.

All types of baskets are made in the factories, but usually they're the wide-splint types, such as picnic baskets; market baskets; baskets for backpacking, sewing, and laundry; and baskets for mail, condiments, wine, berries, garden, harvest, pies and cake, and ladies' handbags.

Fans

Prior to the invention of electric fans, and long before air conditioning was a gleam in the inventor's eye, people used fans, the kind they worked themselves in an effort to stay cool. They spent most of each Sunday in church, and the same church that could be so cold in winter could be miserably hot in summer. So the communicants used small tin or soapstone heaters in winter, and fans in summer.

Later, there would be cardboard ad-

Mountain-made oak-splint fan (left) and round ash-splint and sweet-grass fan (right). Left, $9–$12; right, $15–$20.

Ash-splint and sweet-grass fan with ribbon bow made for the Maine tourist trade around 1915. 9" dia. $18–$30

vertising fans, but in those early days, the ladies and some of the gentlemen depended on Oriental fans if they could afford them. If they couldn't, or just wanted to save money, they made their own fans. In the South, they made fans of palm leaves; in the mountains, they used oak splints; and in the Northeast, round fans made of ash splints were a favorite. Oftentimes, the latter was made of a combination of ash splints and sweet grass. The fragrance of the sweet grass would last for years and was very pleasant when fanned across one's face.

Some of the fans were works of art, because the maker put forth her best efforts, knowing all the other ladies in church would see her workmanship on the finished product. Other beautiful fans were made by Indians of the Northeast, to be sold to the summer visitors who would use them as they sat on the porches around the big hotels.

Fasteners

Ways of fastening basket lids and covers vary with the whims and ability of each maker. Some used rings made of the same material as the basket, made to fasten over a protruding woven piece. Others made a wide weave in the lid and carved a crude fastener to put in it. Some of the baskets have no fasteners—the weight of the lid holds it in place.

Ash-splint feather basket. 13½" dia, 12" o.h. $135–$195

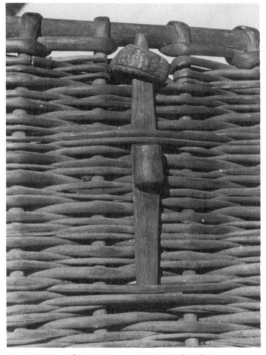

A primitive fastener on a picnic basket.

Feather Basket

Before there were ready-made mattresses, each household made its own. These were usually made from corn shucks, straw, or feathers. Feathers were plentiful, but since much work was involved in securing them, they soon became a status symbol—a homemaker was known and praised for the number of feather beds she owned. Some beds were stuffed so full of feathers they might be 12 to 15 inches high when sunned and fluffed.

The homemaker deserved praise for her feather beds, because feathers weren't as easy to obtain as one might think. Duck, chicken, turkey, and eagle feathers could be used, but goose down was the most desirable. It was also the most difficult to acquire—naturally the geese, which were raised for producing down, were very upset about having their feathers plucked. A basketry contraption was made to fit over the goose's head during plucking, so the plucker had to hold a basket over the goose's head while plucking and at the same time deposit the feathers and down in the feather basket.

The feather basket was made to help as much as possible. The lid was fastened around the handles so it could be raised and lowered easily, without being knocked off. Feather baskets were made of all kinds of splints, but the most desirable ones now are the ones made of ash splints.

Fifties Basketry

Through the years, basketry has experienced revivals, and it has survived slumps when only the very dedicated continued to make a few baskets. There was a major revival around the turn of the century, another

Rattan basket and tray with plywood bottom. Both made in the Fifties. $5–$10

Old finely woven miniature splint basket. 3" dia, 1¾" h. $60–$75

Same basket with small thread for comparison with splints.

around 1938, and still another in the 1950s, with the present revival overshadowing anything that has happened before.

The Fifties revival wasn't nearly as strong as the present revival. Boy Scout and Girl Scout troops were taught the basics of basketmaking, church groups taught the fundamentals to children in summer Bible classes, and adult members made basketry items to be sold in fall bazaars. And, it was common, during that time, for young housewives to get together to make baskets, trays, and other basketry items for their homes.

With the increased interest in things from the Fifties, it's not surprising that some of those baskets are showing up in antique shops, malls, and yard sales.

Finely Woven Baskets

The weaving of baskets could very appropriately be classified into about half a dozen categories. There are several classes of loosely woven baskets just as there are several types of finely woven ones. The majority of baskets will have average weaving,

but those with super-fine splints woven closely are hard to find.

The majority of the finely woven baskets are small, as it takes much more time to make a small fine-woven basket than a large, average weave basket. Since the actual number of finely woven baskets is much less than the number of other types, they are more difficult to find. The finely woven baskets were probably made as gifts or when the basketmaker was experimenting. Makers were probably lucky to get 25 cents for them.

Finishes for Baskets

Many of the new baskets made today, especially the pine needle baskets made by the white basketmakers, are finished with a solution of lacquer that makes them very stiff and hard. They are totally unlike the soft, flexible pine needle baskets made by the Indians. Through the years, some of the basketmakers have varnished, painted, and lacquered their new baskets, but the majority were left natural.

Now that baskets are so much a part of modern decor—they're used in the home rather than in the pantry or barn—a finish might be nice in some cases, but generally they are nicer when left natural. Some collectors claim a finish keeps them from becoming dry and brittle.

To avoid brittleness, some basket collectors put their baskets outside on a regular basis, letting them stay out in the rain for a week or so, while others prefer spraying them with varnish or lacquer. Another method that is chosen by many to preserve and add life to their baskets is to give them an application of about three parts linseed oil to one part turpentine.

If none of the above appeals to you, it does add life to baskets to take them outside annually and spray them with water.

Firewood Baskets

As late as 1925, many homes did all their cooking and heating with wood-burning stoves (this was especially true in rural homes). Even when oil, gas, and electricity became available, many people continued to use wood—it was plentiful, cheap, and they were accustomed to it.

Once the wood was cut and brought home, it was stored in barns and sheds around the house until it was needed. Then it was carried into the house where it was put in woodboxes. For the parlor, the woodbox might only be filled once a week. On Sunday, a woven firewood basket was used. It might be factory-made or handmade. Hand-

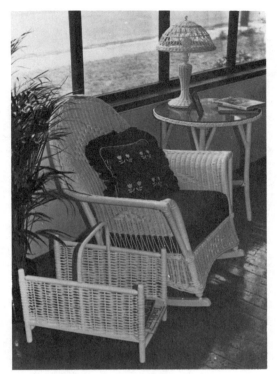

Firewood basket being used as a magazine basket in a room of wicker. $53–$74

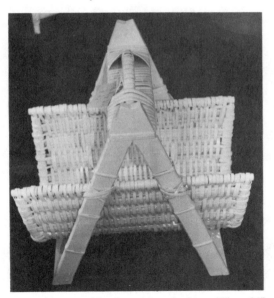

Fancy firewood basket painted white. 18" w, 21" h. $48–$87

Oak-splint firewood basket. $47–$82

Natural woven-splint firewood basket. 20″ l, 19″ h. $29–$39

made firewood baskets were, and still are, the most desirable. The logs were placed neatly in the firewood basket to be used in the fancy parlor heater.

When other types of heat were finally accepted, the firewood baskets were relegated to the basement where they were discovered by basket collectors. Modern collectors had all but ignored the old firewood baskets until the gas crunch of the 1970s. Then, they began looking for them to again hold firewood—this time for woodburning stoves being installed. When fossil fuels became plentiful again, these baskets lost some of their appeal, but they're now being used as magazine racks.

There's only a hair's difference in basketry and wicker; in fact, in the early days, wicker was referred to as *basket furniture.* Today, many of the old firewood baskets cross the line and can be either basketry or wicker accessories.

Fish Basket, Bamboo

The owner says this fish basket or net was used in Vietnam where the user dropped it over a school of fish and then dipped them out through the hole in the top. It was used something like the big nets the American fishermen used half a century ago when they threw the net out like a big skirt in the water.

Vietnamese bamboo fish basket or net. 36″ dia, 17″ h. $50–$75

Fish Traps

Basketmakers used whatever materials were available to make fish traps. In the southern part of the United States, a few basket fish traps can still be found. The old ones are made of oak and hickory splints. No doubt, river cane and swamp cane were used if basketmakers thought the cane would work. In the northern part of the country, roots seemed to be the favorite material.

The fish traps are similar to the eel traps, as they were designed along the same lines— to lure in fish but make it impossible for them to get out.

Southern-made oak-splint fish trap. 17" dia, 4' 3" h. $125–$215

Willow fish trap used in the Northeast. 19" dia bottom, 40" h. $99–$135

Five-Cent Baskets

It was the custom in that long-ago era of the summer tourist heyday, when the sale of baskets and basketry items all but supported the family, for the mother to keep the children near her. She couldn't afford a baby-sitter so it was necessary for her to keep the children with her. In an effort to keep the children busy, and therefore more manageable, parents taught the children to make baskets, small ones at first. The Abenakis lead the field in this endeavor.

The first baskets were small, plain, and easily made. The children would quickly master the craft and would either go on to making larger and better baskets or would find they preferred another line of work. So, the five-cent baskets served a dual role—

Five-cent basket has all the earmarks of a beginning basketmaker. 2" dia, 3½" o.h. $5–$9

Flower-gathering basket. $17–$32

they were a form of baby-sitter and, as the baskets were sold, the children learned the value of free enterprise.

Five-Leaf Ivy

The name *five-leaf ivy* was used for Virginia Creeper in an effort to distinguish it from poison ivy. Virginia Creeper has a five-part leaf; poison ivy only has three. See "Virginia Creeper."

Flag

Flag is the name given any of a number of plants that grow in marshes and bogs. It has sword-shaped leaves, and different species have different colored blossoms, including blue, purple, yellow, and white. See "Rush" and "Cattails."

Flower-Gathering Baskets

Flower-gathering baskets were usually round with slightly curved sides where the handle was attached. They came in several differ-

ent sizes, but all were made to accommodate long stems. Most were made of either willow, reed, or rattan, while a few made of oak, hickory, and ash splints have been found.

Today, flower-gathering baskets are used more for magazine holders and fruit and vegetable displays than for gathering flowers.

Flower-Pot Cuffs

Recently, there has been a revival of the use of greenery in the home. In the early part of this century, there was another revival. Then (as now) plants weren't left in plain flower pots; they were either put in fancy brass pots or the pots were covered in some other way, sometimes by woven cuffs called *flower-pot cuffs*.

Plain cuffs were made over cardboard or brown paper for a pleasing effect. Types listed in instruction books included braided grass in loops, cuffs trimmed with buttonholes, tied rush over matting, and knotted cuffs with buttonholed edges.

They were fragile, inexpensive things that were discarded when no longer needed, but this writer remembers them from childhood. A diligent search failed to uncover one for an illustration, but directions can be found in old basketry instruction books. A medium-sized pot required a circle or cuff 5 to 6 inches in diameter and 6 to 7 inches tall.

Folded Squares

Another name for the diamond that covers the "join" where the handle fastens into the body of the basket. It makes the basket more attractive and reinforces the handle. See "God's Eye."

Forms or Molds for Baskets

In the Deep South, and in the mountains of Tennessee, Kentucky, and into Missouri, basket forms or molds were seldom used—basketmakers fashioned their baskets as they made them. In the northern states, however, especially New England, nearly everyone used forms for shaping their baskets.

A basketmaker might have dozens of forms or molds in assorted sizes. Basket forms were also used to make the now-famous Nantucket Lightship basket, as well as the many ash and sweet-grass baskets made by New Englanders, including the Penobscots, Passamaquoddies, Micmacs, and Maliseets. The Shakers also used basket forms. The basket forms shown in the illustration belonged to the grandmother of a Penobscot lady who taught a basketry class on the reservation at Old Town, Maine.

Three basket molds and two cutters for ash splints. Molds, $75–$115; cutters, $35–$63

Unusual basket mold or form due to the fact that it was made to fit one person's needs. The basketmaker wanted to make a tall, slender basket and be able to hold the mold between his or her knees, if necessary. $50–$65

Fountain

The same over and under weaving that is used to make baskets is used to make wicker, but generally the wicker is a more refined version. The fountain (shown in the photograph) is thought to have been used in one of the luxury hotels during, or maybe shortly before the Roaring Twenties, and is a good example of refined over and under weaving. It is included here to show just how refined weaving can be.

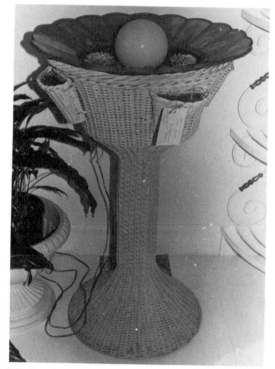

Wicker fountain. 27" dia, 40" h. $2000–$3500

There is a light in the center as well as a pump in the bottom that allowed the fountain to work. This formed a water base on which fresh flowers were placed.

Freehand-Design Painting

Potato or block painting was done by dipping a potato, turnip, or other block into dye, and then stamping the design on the

Freehand-decorated basket. 12" w, 13" l, 4½" h.
$48–$85

weavers of the basket. Another type of decoration was the freehand-design painting. Several tribes of Indians, including the Algonquian, used this method of basket decoration in the early days. Instead of using the potato or block, they painted freehand dots and crosses on the basket. The designs may not be exactly alike from one weaver to the next, but they are similar.

French-Made Baskets

Collectors assembled at an auction where these baskets and an assortment of others were being sold failed to identify these— one lady thought they may have come from France because she had seen baskets like them while visiting there.

They are attractive and well made. The rims of the baskets and the covers are nailed on, and the swing handle attached with a metal fastener. The handles are unlike those found on American-made baskets in that they are rounded on the edges, and the handles are only about half the width of typical American basket handles. Both sold for the same price—$155 each.

Tall splint basket. $125–$175

Squatty splint basket. $125–$175

Friendship Basket, Taghkanic

Originally these baskets were called fruit baskets, but through the years the name has been changed, and they are now known as friendship baskets. They are especially strong due to the double handles begin lashed together so they can hold a considerable amount of weight.

The older ones were made of ash splints, a favorite of New England and New York basketmakers, but as the availability of good ash trees decreased, they began to be made of maple, maybe other woods as well.

Taghkanic friendship basket. 12" dia, 2" h.
$200–$300

Froe

The *froe,* a cleaving tool with a handle at right angles to the blade, is more closely associated with shingle making than basketmaking, but many old basketmakers found it invaluable in making oak splints for baskets.

Fruit Gift Baskets

Shippers of gift fruits have long used baskets. The bright colors of the fruit against the white woven basket is very impressive. One firm—Harry and David of Medford, Oregon—realized that fact long ago and has been shipping gift fruit baskets since.

Fruit basket made in 1951. $13\frac{1}{4}$" l, 10" w, 16" o.h.
$10–$22

Now the company's empty hand-woven baskets are turning up in flea markets and antique malls. They're easily identified as each is stamped on the bottom with the company name and the information that they were "handwoven and packed" by Harry and David. A check with the company revealed that it is probably the largest handwoven-basket factory in the country. No doubt, it uses a more or less assembly-line production basis. The baskets have wooden bottoms, which is essential for holding the weight of the fruit.

"Fully Dressed" Basket

Today motorcycle owners want their bikes "fully dressed," that is, they want lots of fancy accessories to transform them from the ordinary to the exotic. Half a century ago some lady felt the same about a factory-made basket. She took a plain peck basket and added a blue cover that also served as a lining. Not content with that, she added a 4½-inch wide row of crocheted lace. The basket's original use is not known, but it would have been perfect to use as a waste-basket beside a wicker desk.

Factory-made peck basket with fabric and lace cover. 10" dia, 7½" h. $19–$33

Fustic

A tropical tree of the mulberry family that is native to America. The wood chips of the fustic tree are used to make yellow dye, but if boiled too long, make a dark green dye.

Gainsborough Basket

Around 1900, in England, this particular type of basket became quite famous under the name of the *Gainsborough* basket. Its popularity spread to America, but apparently its name was lost in the shuffle. It was used here just as it was there—to hold freshly cut flowers in flower shops and in flower shows. But as homes grew smaller after World War II, the large arrangement lost much of its appeal. People simply preferred a smaller basket of flowers.

Although it was used into the 1950s, it never again reached the popularity it had known around the turn of the century. Today, examples of the Gainsborough basket are included in some basket collections simply to show the range of styles.

The Gainsborough basket. 14" w, 29" o.h. $10–$25

Gathering Baskets

Although most baskets were used for gathering something—anything from food and eggs to flowers—this one was always referred to as a gathering basket, according to the tag attached to it. It is made of ash splints and is round and well made.

Half-bushel gathering basket with stationary handle. $350–$450

Factory-made oak gathering basket. 12" w, 20" l, 9½" o.h. $35–$44

One of the most difficult tasks for basket collectors is to try to determine the use and maker of a basket. We have to think back to a time where there were no cardboard boxes and no paper or plastic bags. Baskets were used for all the chores bags are used for today. There was less demand for containers back then because people grew much of what they ate. But that food still had to be planted and harvested.

A large family would have dozens of baskets, some probably made by members of the family, others bought from a neighbor or a traveling basketmaker. Gathering baskets came in many sizes and shapes. Which type of basket was chosen for a particular chore depended on what was being gathered, and by whom.

Gauge, Hand-held

Since the poplar strips used to weave the covers for the fancy boxes made by the Shakers had to be exact and almost perfect, the first person to cut those strips back in 1869 had to have good eyesight and steady hands.

The poplar strips or splints had to be cut one-eighth of an inch in width. Shortly after the Shakers began cutting the splints, one of the brethren devised a hand-held gauge. It was a small piece of wood with teeth set in one end, one-eighth of an inch apart. A piece of flexible metal was attached to the top and held the poplar in place while it was pulled through the teeth. This was not difficult as the strips of poplar were paper thin.

This method was not entirely satisfactory, and in 1872 one of the brethren designed and made a steam-powered gauge that continued to be used as long as the boxes were made.

Another gauge has been found that can't be identified as belonging to any person or group because the teeth are completely worn away. It is quite similar to the hand-held Shaker gauge but has a strong wire across the top.

Hand-held Shaker gauge. 4½" l, ⅝" w. $28–$55

Gauge with wire. 4½" l, ⅝" w. $25–$50

Gift Basket

There is little difference between gift baskets and fruit gift baskets, except in the making. Fruit gift baskets are made by the company to hold fruits that will be shipped as a gift, while the gift basket will be carefully and lovingly made by one person to give to another. Of course, in earlier days the gift basket might come complete with a gift—maybe home-grown fruit, vegetables, or even needlework—but always in the case of the gift basket, the basket itself was of utmost importance.

With the present revival of basketmaking, the custom is being revived. Beautiful baskets are being made and given to friends and family. The new baskets may be filled with scented soaps or jams and jellies, homemade or bought. A basket, old or new, filled with a deck of playing cards, some paperback books, or maybe a few snacks makes a welcome gift for a shut-in.

Gizzard Basket

Another name for the buttocks basket. So-called because of the indented center rib. See "Buttocks Basket."

Glass Baskets

Like Cinderella's slipper, both shoes and baskets were made of glass by glass companies, for a decade or so. Several types

Glass basket. 2" w, 4" l, 5" o.h. $14–$18

were made, but this one, which is one of the simpler examples, utilizes the woven basketry idea well.

Glass and Brass Basket

Decorative baskets were extremely popular a century or so ago, to fill the many whatnots in Victorian homes. The holly scene makes the one shown here especially attractive for use at Christmas. It could also be used year-round for nuts and candy.

Brass basket with white glass insert. 5" dia, 6" o.h. $35–$55

God's Eye

The majority of old basketmakers kept their baskets plain, simple, and sturdy, except for the occasional basket that would be used for shopping or as a gift. These they usually "fancied up" a bit.

They often used what is now commonly known as a *God's eye* or folded square to reinforce the handle where it joined the basket. Making the square of splints, whether of cane, oak, ash, or some other material, required a certain amount of expertise. It is still used today by modern basketmakers. It is sometimes called "diamonds."

Rattan covered basket with God's eye. $25–$45

Goldenback Fern

Goldenback is a fern that grows along the East Coast and was often used as a substitute for maidenhair fern stems, which it closely resembles.

Golden Ragwort

The foliage of this wild plant of the thistle family is smooth and thin and, along with its stalk, is often slightly shaded to purple on the end. The rest of the long tough leaves and stalks are white, which gives the plant an unusual but lovely effect when used in coiled baskets. Another name for this plant is *squaw grass.*

Goldthread

Goldthread is an evergreen plant, *Coptis trifolia,* whose roots yield a clear, bright, lasting yellow. Dye from this plant was used in basketry, and its roots were used in medicine. See "Yellow" under "Dyes."

Goose Basket

Long ago, a good homemaker was known by the number of feather beds in her home—with good down topping the list. To rise to the top of the social ladder in any community, she had to continue plucking geese and making feather beds.

A live goose whose feathers and down were plucked without the benefit of a sedative could get quite angry, and it's only recourse was pecking the picker. But housewives looking for both comfort and social status had to keep plucking, so for protection they bought goose baskets.

These baskets were made to fit over the head of the goose to prevent it from pecking. Some were made wider at the bottom

Straight-splint goose basket painted white. 10" dia, 22" h. $65–$98

to accommodate the goose's shoulders, while others were made about the same size from bottom to top. The baskets are long and narrow, and the goose was put in the basket headfirst.

Some baskets were made to serve an additional purpose: Covers were made for the goose baskets which were used to store feathers and down until they could be used in mattresses and pillows.

Like many handmade items, goose baskets can be found in different sizes and shapes. Those from the South are mostly made of oak splints, while those from the Northeast are mostly made of ash splints.

"Granny's Fanny" Basket

Just another name someone coined for the peculiar-shaped but well-known buttocks or gizzard basket. See "Buttocks Baskets."

Grapevine

Both wild and cultivated grapevines were used in basketry. They were often mixed with other vines, especially muscadine. Un-

Miniature grapevine baskets made by the Cherokees. $10–$15

like so many other vines and ground runners, the roots of grapevines were also used, especially in weaving. New baskets coming in from the Philippines now have roots showing along the vines or ground runners, indicating they are probably grape or kudzu.

During the first half of this century, Boy Scouts were taught basketry as part of their woods and field training. It is safe to assume they used more grapevines in their baskets than any other kind, because they were easier to find.

Grass Twine

Hong Kong grass was also known by this name. See "Hong Kong Grass."

Grocery Store Baskets

Factory-made baskets like these are believed to have first been used in turn-of-the-century grocery stores, initially for display and later as delivery baskets. Grocery orders could be dropped off at the store by the husband on his way to work. (Later they were called in on that fancy new contraption, the telephone.) The groceries would be put in a basket, and the delivery boy would take it to the customer's house.

Later delivery boys had bicycles with large baskets fastened on the front and back. These were necessary as the orders were getting larger and the neighborhood expanding. Still later these old wooden splint

Factory-made grocery basket. 15" w, 30" l, 16" h. $32–$44

baskets were used for laundry, or for carrying the baby in the car.

Gullah Baskets

Background

The *Gullah,* or Afro-American-made, baskets are famous all over the United States. These baskets have probably been made using the same method for centuries. The Gullahs still make baskets exactly like their African ancestors.

Fortunately, their ancestors found almost the same type basket materials in America in the late 1600s. Although they lived in slavery on the plantations of South Carolina's Low Country, Afro-Americans continued to make baskets like their ancestors. The men made work baskets to be used

The Gullah baskets on the left are old; those on the right are new. $12–$25 each

Materials used in Gullah baskets.

The grass is coiled, and then sewn together with palmetto strips.

on the plantations and in their own homes, and the women made pretty show baskets for use around the house, for gifts, or for selling.

Records from some of the old plantations show that as early as 1730, the black slaves were making and using *fanner* baskets for cleaning and winnowing rice. Fanning rice was a method similar to one used in West Africa. After the rice was harvested, it was put in a wooden mortar and pounded with a wooden pestle. This broke the hulls but didn't remove them from the rice. The rice then had to be taken from the mortar to a large and almost flat coiled basket where it was thrown into the air (fanned) until the hulls or husks were removed from the grains.

This craft has been handed down from mother to daughter and father to son for generations. Although few work baskets are made now, both boys and girls are taught to make them. During the last half century, this sort of basketmaking has developed into a rather lucrative business. Basketmakers now have stands along the highways that afford them a chance to show and sell their baskets while allowing them to take care of their homes and children. Many of these stands are located on U.S. Highway 60, in the community of Mt. Pleasant, just outside of Charleston, South Carolina.

Incidentally, Gullah is a language of more than one race of people, but it has been used so long in connection with Low Country baskets that they are best known as Gullah baskets.

Seldom are more than one of the four basic Gullah materials—sea grass (often called sea straw by the workers), bull rush, pine needles, and palmetto—used in any one basket. A tougher rush or grass called *rushel* is now being used in some of their baskets. Pine needles are added more for color than as a material.

The Gullah people have recently taken advantage of modern appliances and now freeze the palmetto before using it. They say this method makes the palmetto last longer and work more easily.

Show Baskets

So-called Gullah show baskets were and still are made of sea grass sewn together with split palmetto (palm) leaves. The use of these two materials makes the baskets light and colorful. Show baskets were first made around 1900. When the coastal highway was paved outside Charleston in the 1920s, women there began selling their baskets in stands outside their homes. Today, there are over 60 family-operated stands on a four-mile stretch of U.S. Highway 17.

Work Baskets

Gullah men always made the work baskets because they had to be tough enough to be used on the farms. To give them great strength, they were made of bull rushes sewn together with thin white oak splints or split palmetto butts. Now there is little to no demand for work baskets, but the men occasionally make the large baskets.

Roadside stand showing variety of Gullah baskets.

Hair Receivers

Hair receivers were made in silver, hand-painted china, glass, celluloid, and basketry. Before the Flapper era, most women wore their hair long. Often they would save the hair left in their combs to make "rats," paddings over which the hair could be combed to give it a "full" effect, similar to the Gibson Girl look. The hair receiver was used to store the hair until enough was collected to make a rat.

Display of baskets. Prices on the new baskets range from $20 to $55 each.

Hair was stuffed through the hole in the top of a hair receiver, and it was opened to take it out. 4" dia, 6" h. $25–$40

98

Ha-kin-ne

As early as 1881, the Zuni (a people of western New Mexico) were making a ring or cover for their heads on which a basket could rest, and they called it a *Ha-kin-ne*. It cushioned the weight of the basket and probably helped to balance it.

Drawing of a Ha-kin-ne.

Half Basket

Half baskets are believed to be strictly a Southern invention. In fact, they could go as far back as the Southern plantation where

Oak-splint half basket painted white. 5½" w, 10½" l, 7½" o.h. Painted, $35–$50; natural, $150–$200.

they were used to keep keys by the door and to store bobbins in the loom room.

Half baskets can be used to store a multitude of different things, because the flat side fits against the wall, eliminating half the width of a regular basket. They also lend themselves to all types of decorating, such as holding arrangements of fresh flowers or of dried flowers and leaves.

Hana-Kago

The Japanese name for baskets made exclusively for flower arranging is *hana-kago*. Long known as leaders in flower arranging, the Japanese made their own baskets, perhaps with the idea that they could be made to complement each other. These baskets were used for *ikebana* (fresh flowers) and for *zokwa* (artificial flowers). It's possible some of the old *hana-kago* are now finding their way into the States since there is so much travel between the two countries.

Hand Basket

When, where, and how the name *hand basket* originated for this type basket is unknown, especially when all baskets were carried by hand. Perhaps it stemmed from the fact country women used it as a sort of

Oak-splint hand basket. 8" w, 10½" l, 9" o.h. $95–$150

handbag, that is, they took it with them when they went shopping—to carry their money to the store and their purchases home.

The term *hand basket* is well known for its presence in the expression "going to hell in a hand basket," which is what my grandfather would say of the country when he became upset over a political situation.

Hand baskets vary a bit in size, but they are all quite similar otherwise. Oak splints were the most popular materials used to make them, but ash and hickory were also used.

Handkerchief Boxes

Basket handkerchief boxes are believed to have been strictly tourist-trade items. While other types may have been made, in the northeast part of the United States, square handkerchief baskets with a center opening were the most popular. Also, ash-splint and sweet-grass handkerchief boxes were made—plain with solid tops that swung open.

Some handkerchief boxes had round lift tops and others had square tops, but all were made of a combination of paper-thin ash splints and sweet grass. Some had narrow

Ash-splint and sweet-grass handkerchief box, Penobscot Museum. $65–$125

Ash-splint and sweet-grass handkerchief box. 7¼" sq, 2¼" h. $55–$90

Ash-splint and sweet-grass handkerchief box, Unity College collection. $65–$100

dyed splints; others had decorations of bows and curlicues made of thin splints.

In those days, a handkerchief was a very necessary part of one's outfit. Handkerchiefs were always fancy, usually with delicate embroidery or a lace border.

Making basketry items for the tourist trade could be quite lucrative. The Abenakis, a Canadian tribe, spent summers in the States making basketry items to be sold at large resorts. One such basketmaker reported an income of over $4000 back in 1910. Of course, she worked all during the winter, and then in summer she hired other basketmakers to help her fill orders and keep her stand stocked.

Handles for Baskets

The old basketmakers, who also carved designs and whittled toys, often made exquisite designs on basket handles. But whether it was fancy or not, the emphasis was always on a strong, sturdy handle—one that was strong enough to carry the weight of the basket and its contents.

Although it was important to have a strong handle, basketmakers emphasized that the handle also had to be graceful and in

Ash-splint basket with a beautifully proportioned handle. $175–$250

Bushel basket of oak splints with good handles. $200–$295

Reinforced handle on bushel basket.

Ash-splint basket with a handle that is too low. $125–$175

Basket with handles on the ends. $40–$70

Identical basket with handles on either side. $40–$70

The handle goes around the basket for strength and reinforcement. $250–$300

proportion with the basket. The type of handle varied with the whims and skills of the maker. Some made rope handles, while others used braided, wrapped, or looped handles. Then there were those who never varied their basketmaking methods or styles; they continued to make good, solid splint handles.

Handles for baskets range from ordinary to elegant, if basket handles can be classified as elegant. Most over-the-top handles are of plain, tough oak, ash, or hickory splints. The handle may have a design carved or whittled on it, or it could be lashed onto the basket quite elegantly. It's interesting

Braided handle.

to find two almost identical baskets with the handles on the sides of one and on the ends of the other. But the ingenuity of our ancestors is never more visible than in the carving and attaching of handles on burden bushel baskets. It was imperative that the handles hold, especially if one were carrying precious seeds or foods; therefore, they not only carved them to fit so their weight would rest on a sturdy point, they also wove the handle into the basket for reinforcement.

Braided Handles

Braided handles were used more on vine and cane baskets, although there are cases where they were used on other types of baskets. The braids could be made of 3, 9, or 12 strands, and were braided like hair. Finely cut splints could be used as could cane, reed, rattan, sweet, and Hong Kong grass.

Ring Handle

The ring handle is exactly what the name implies—a fancy ring made of the same material as that used in the basket. Generally

Ring handle on side of ash-splint basket.

ring handles are made more for appearance than for service. They are found on the sides of baskets and are used as fasteners for lids.

Rope Handles

Rope handles were not made of rope per se. The rope handle described by basketmaking instructors was made by wrapping a long, fine weaver around a thin, round foundation rod. This made it look like a rope; hence, the name *rope handle*. The weavers could be wrapped solidly or widely spaced in sections, or even in three or four coils together at intervals the length of the handle.

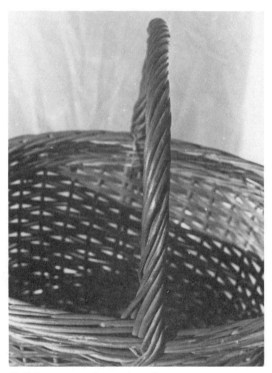

Solidly wrapped rope handle.

Twisted Handle

As the name implies, a *twisted handle* is simply a handle that's been twisted. The handle could consist of several small pieces of reed or rattan, or it might be strips of cane. The twisted handle can easily be confused with a rope handle. Some baskets are found with a single twist; others have a double twist.

Woven Handle

Some basketmakers have always made fancy handles on their baskets. Some even carved beautiful designs on the solid wood handles. Others fancied up the handles by weaving over the plain handles or by adding a woven handle.

Oak-splint basket with weaving over plain handle. 7" w, 8" l, 9" o.h. $50–$60

Wrapped Handle

The biggest difference between the rope and the wrapped handle is that the wrapped handle usually has more than one rod in its foundation, and it is wrapped solidly from one end to the other. Also, wrapped handles are fancier. Some of the old basketmakers often put a wooden rod, like a small handle, on the bottom of the wrapped handle, and then wrapped it to give it a three-prong effect. This was called a *bracing rod*.

Hanging Baskets

Ornamental

Any basketmaker working with long pine needles is apt to try different ways of coiling the needles into something interesting and decorative. This is especially true of the Coushatta Indians of Louisiana who have a history of making unusual pine needle basketry items. One unusual item is a wall-hanging in the shape of a cup and saucer. In the Northeast, the Indians made another type of wall hanging—a circle with a tall, staggered top.

Coushatta-made pine needle wall hanging. 7"h, 8" w. $18–$25

Plant Holder

The heavier-than-usual cord or small rope around this basket formed a three-sectioned hanger so the basket could be hung. It appears to date from around 1920 and was made in several sizes.

Penobscot-made ash-splint and sweet-grass wall hanging, Unity College collection. $38–$54

Rattan

So far no one has been able to come up with a use for this basket. It is very large for a hanging type, yet not strong enough to hold much weight. Nor are the small, braided twine hangers strong enough to support much weight.

Before weaving began, the rattan was dyed a dark blue—the twine hangers were dyed an even darker blue. Both were done with commercial dyes. The basket must have hung in or near a window, causing about a third of the basket to fade considerably from the light.

Hanging rattan basket. $17\frac{1}{2}''$ dia, $9\frac{1}{2}''$ h. $65–$105

Willow hanging plant holder. 6'' dia, $5\frac{1}{2}''$ h. $11–$19

Hats

Straw hats are believed to have come in vogue around summer theatres. Regardless of where it started, the craze soon spread across the country. Early in the twentieth century, few men dared to go out in the summer without wearing a Panama straw hat.

Derby powder-puff box, Unity College collection. $37–$56

The flat-topped style straw hat became known as a *skimmer* when worn by the men, and a *sailor* when worn by women. In resort areas, men wore white pants, blue blazers, and straw hats, while the ladies wore white embroidered dresses and sailor straw hats.

Basketmakers in those areas took notice and designed small souvenir-type basketry hats. All were made of sweet grass and paper-thin splints of ash. The ladies' hats were made in two pieces; when the top is removed, there is a place to store her powder puff.

Sailor hat powder-puff box. 6½" dia, 3" h. $40–$62

Hazelwood

The hazel tree has served many purposes: It grows delicious hazelnuts, or filberts; it was used in wooden-boat building; and the wood is so light and flexible, it's perfect for basketmaking. All hazel wood is light; in fact, it's so light, the Hupa Indians used it to make most of their burden baskets. The branches or shoots could be used for both the spokes and weavers.

Heels

In some areas of the country this name was used for the reinforcement strips on the bottom of baskets. See "Runners."

Hen Basket

Before the advent of electricity and incubators, it was the custom among farm folk to let the old hen lay a nest of eggs and then let her "set" on them until the chicks hatched. Some hens would raise one nest of chicks and immediately start on another. They were known as *broody hens*—good broody hens.

Not all hens were good broody hens, and the ones who were, were treasured—and loaned. A family with only one or two good broody hens might borrow a broody hen or two from a neighbor, after the neighbor had enough young chicks for her family.

Hen basket. 8" w, 13" l, 13" o.h. $39–$54

In a basketmaking society it was only natural that baskets would be made especially to transport hens back and forth. Hen baskets could also be used to take fryers or hens who were no longer laying many eggs to the general store to be sold or traded for things like coffee, sugar, salt, and spices.

This type basket actually originated in Europe, and the people immigrating here brought the idea with them. The basket is believed to have originated in Scandinavia, although there is still some question about it. For the most part, these baskets weren't called broody hen baskets in the Old Country. There they were called by different names, usually depending on the country. In Sweden the basket was known as the *Scottish basket,* and it was always used to transport hens. The basketmakers of Kilmuir in Skye made so many of the baskets that in some places they became known as *Skye hen baskets. Ose baskets* is another name, and it comes from osier (willow), as the early ones were all made of willow. Years ago they were also made in Hungary and Yugoslavia, as well as in Sicily, where they were used for fish.

Hemlock

Hemlock trees are found from Nova Scotia to Alabama. Hemlock wood has been used widely and in many different ways by basketmakers, since it adjusts easily to fit the needs of the makers. For basketmakers, the most important part of the tree is the roots, which are usually split before being used.

Herb Basket, Contemporary

No record has been found of an herb basket of this design being made prior to the past five years. For years the Indians made a similar basket and called it an elbow basket, so there is every possibility that they were made earlier. We do know that from the time the Pilgrims arrived, herbs have been grown and used profusely.

Contemporary oak-splint herb basket. Opening 5" w, 7" l, 17" o.h. $13–$18

These baskets are now being made by contemporary basketmakers here and in the Philippines. They are quite useful for dried flowers as well as herbs.

Hexagon Weave

Most basketmakers, regardless of location, used the hexagon or honeycomb weave. This weave may have originated with cheese baskets, most of which were made using the

Hexagon-weave basket. 18" dia, 14" h. $25–$45

107

Wide split-cane hanging basket with hexagon weave, late. 11" h, 10½" by 7½" opening. $15–$24

hexagon weave, but its use is not restricted to cheese baskets. You'll find many different types of baskets with a hexagon weave.

Hickey Baskets

The first name of this old basketmaker is unknown. Earlier in this century, people in eastern Tennessee would seek out a man named Hickey who came each spring with a load of beautiful, well-made willow baskets. If an individual didn't have the money

Hickey-made willow basket with handles on either side. Private collection. $75–$95

to purchase one of Mr. Hickey's baskets, he would trade them for chickens, eggs, or another commodity.

Hickory Splint

The hickory tree, a member of the walnut family, is one of America's toughest trees. It has been used to make cane chairs, destined for rough-and-tough service, usually in families with many children.

Hickory splints have never been as popular as oak splints for making spokes and weavers. They were, however, very popular for making basket handles because they were tough and durable.

The way the handle is attached is a trademark of Hickey baskets. $85–$115

Well-made hickory-splint basket. 19" dia, 13" h. $110–$150

Hines, Regina

Contemporary Georgia basketmaker who has perfected the art of *kudzu vine* basketmaking. Now teaches her craft in area colleges.

Hip Basket

Another name for the *gizzard* or *buttocks* basket. People using baskets had a tendency to call them by simple names, ones that usually applied to the way they would be used. This type of basket fit comfortably on the hip, making it easy to carry; hence the name. See "Buttocks Basket."

Holy Grass

Holy grass is just another name for the sweet grass that was and still is used by the Indians of the Northeast to make baskets. It acquired the name *holy grass* many, many years ago in Europe where it was scattered in front of the churches, probably to make a path through the snow or mud or to release its fragrance. It was also placed along paths leading to religious shrines.

Hominy Sieve

When white men arrived in the New World, the Indians introduced them to corn or maize. In fact, the Indians went so far as to teach the newcomers how to grow and cook it because they knew that without it, chances of survival were slim They had a few squash and pumpkins, but corn was the staple, the one they could depend on for survival. The same food served day after day becomes monotonous; therefore, they were always searching for new ways to cook it.

Not a new way of eating corn, but one they seemed to like, was hominy. Making hominy was done by putting dried, shelled corn into a basket and boiling it in water heated by hot rocks. Some cooked it in hot ashes that had been leached out to become

Swamp-cane hominy sieve. 15" sq, 4" h. $55–$75

lye. The next step was removing the ashes and hulls. This was done by shaking the corn vigorously in a hominy sieve. Some Indian tribes washed their hominy in the sieve, while others made a basketry corn washer for this job. In the South the Sieves were made of cane, while in other areas oak, ash, and hickory splints were used.

Honeycomb Weave

Another name for hexagon weave. See Hexagon Weave.

Honeysuckle Vine

Many vines can be used to make baskets, but probably none is more widely used than honeysuckle. Its popularity can be attributed to the fact that honeysuckle grows wild all over the country. The Cherokees used vines more often than anyone else (with the possible exception of mountain basketmakers).

Care must be taken when gathering this vine. Cherokees insist that the honeysuckle, or any other vine used in basketry, be gathered in the fall. Only the past year's growth should be taken. Vines that have been allowed to grow for several years will have small branches growing on them, and when removed, will leave rough places that detract from the smoothness of the vine. Vines may be used alone or combined with splints to make baskets. Any of the vines can be dyed.

Covered splint and honeysuckle basket, Unity College collection. $45–$65

Hong Kong Grass

Half a century or so ago, the Chinese devised a method of twisting sea grass while it was held under water. This technique re-

Yarn basket of Hong Kong grass and ash splints. 7" dia, 11" h. $39–$58

Lift-top box made of Hong Kong grass and ash splints has a sweet-grass border. 4½" sq, 2½" h. $25–$44

sulted in a product closely resembling small rope.

Hong Kong grass was imported for use in both basketmaking and chair caning. It was very popular because it was handmade and fit right into the scheme of handmade baskets. It was also very inexpensive.

Knowledge of basketry and basketry materials is essential to distinguish between the braided and twisted sweet grass used by the Indians of the Northeast and imported Hong Kong grass. These two types of grasses were often combined in one basket.

It was much easier to use Hong Kong grass, because it didn't have to be gathered and dyed. It could be bought in red, green, blue, brown, orange, and natural. It sold in 3- and 4-pound *hanks,* with each hank consisting of approximately 300 feet of twisted sweet grass.

Collection of baskets

Picnic baskets

(l to r) Small splint, bushwhacker, half-bushel, and freehand-designed baskets

Block- or potato-printed bonnet basket

Three small Nantucket baskets

Plain ash-splint storage basket

Ash-splint storage basket

Assortment of baskets

(l to r) Peach basket, storage basket, and feather basket

Collection of small basketry items

Moose-hair embroidered birch-bark box

Porcupine quill boxes and beaded baskets

From the Unity College Collection of baskets

From the Unity College Collection of baskets

From the Unity College Collection of baskets

From the Unity College Collection of baskets

Urn-shaped wastebasket, ash splint and Hong Kong grass with sweet-grass border, 8½" dia, 11½" h. $30–$49

Basket cover of Hong Kong grass and ash splints, with a center of sweet grass. Cover only: 9½" dia, 2½" h. $10–$15

The natural color was a beautiful beige or tan that blended in perfectly with paper-thin ash splints. It was used in large amounts when making tourist-trade items. Hong Kong grass was also called *grass twine*.

Hopi wickerwork peach basket. 10½" dia, 9½" h. $200–$350

Hopi Indians

Today, about three-fourths of the 10,000 members of the Hopi tribe live on the 641,000-acre Hopi reservation in Arizona. The name *Hopi* is derived from the Shoshone language and means "peaceful ones." They call themselves *Moqui,* and they are basically farmers.

Peaches are one of the better Hopi crops, and apparently always have been. Government reports from the 1800s on Indian affairs often have pictures of peach baskets, usually identified as Hopi peach baskets. Many tribes raised peaches, but none with the prestige and flair of the Hopi, whose trees were originally sent to them by Queen Isabella of Spain.

The Hopi made very fine peach baskets, but their basketry extended beyond that. They were, and still are, well known for their excellent basketry of all types. Like their Indian neighbors in the Southwest, the Hopi made coiled and wickerwork trays and baskets of rabbit brush, sumac, wild currant bush, and yucca. And like their basketmaking neighbors, they wove designs in their baskets—designs representing their dreams, surroundings, and religion.

Horse-Feeding Basket

Long ago, when people had to depend on horses for transportation, they took good care of their horses, whether riding them or driving them hitched to the wagon or carriage. In those days horses were so treasured that it was a hanging crime to steal one. Horse owners always carried grain to feed their horses, especially if they would be away from home or unable to get to a stable in town. The only problem was that so much grain would be wasted if it weren't put in a container or trough. At this point the basketmaker's ingenuity came into play. The basketmaker designed and made a basket that could be partially filled with grain and hung over a horse's head. Both oak and ash splints were used to make these baskets.

Horse-feeding basket. 13" dia, 13" h. **$75–$125**

Ash-splint horse-feeding basket made by the Maliseet Indians. 12" dia, 13" h. **$125–$195**

Huckleberry

There is hardly a tree, shrub, vine, or grass that can't be used in basketry. In the early days of basketmaking basketmakers used whatever was available, even if they had to experiment with materials that had never been used before.

The name *huckleberry* is believed to be a corruption of the word *hurtleberry*. The huckleberry bush bears a dark blue or black edible berry, and its young, slender, flexible limbs were used in basketry.

Huck-Muck

Back in the days when a man could make a little beer for his own use, and later, when it was illegal and he made it just the same, he used a basketry item called a "huck-muck." A huck-muck was used to strain the beer. The huck-muck originated in England and was a 7-to-9-inch tall basketry item that looked a little like a miniature woven back pack. It was placed inside a keg or barrel, and when the tap was turned on, it strained the beer.

There are several reasons why huck-mucks are seldom seen today, except in old books. They were always wet, which caused some deterioration. Also, since they served no other purpose, they were discarded or destroyed when no longer needed. They were woven with willow osiers.

Iizuka Hosia

Around the turn of the century, Iizuka Hosia was one of the best-known Tokyo basket-makers.

Indian Currant

This plant is also called coralberry, coral bush, and buckbush (a name given to it by mountain basketmakers who probably weren't aware of other names). Indian currant is a shrub of the honeysuckle family used as a basketry material in the southern and eastern states. Once the vines have been cleaned and peeled, it's difficult to distinguish between Indian currant and honeysuckle. It's not unusual for basketmakers to mix several types of vines in one basket.

Indigo

Indigo is a plant used to make blue dyes for such things as fabric and basket materials. The most commonly cultivated species of this plant in America is *indigofera tinctoria*. It's a shrub-type plant that grows to heights of 3 and 4 feet.

Oldtimers kept a dye pot, usually indigo, ready at all times. It was used to dye wool for both clothing and coverlets. In the South and Midwest, indigo was used more sparingly on baskets, but in the Northeast it was used extensively on both wool yarns and basket materials.

The shades of blue will vary, as the color depends on the strength of dye used when the material was dyed. Sometimes the dye was first used on wools or splints, and then the leftover was used on basket materials.

This dye was easy to prepare and easy to apply. In fact, it was very easy to apply using the Indian method of swabbing one side of the ash splint with a piece of fabric or the soft skin of an animal. The paper-thin ash splints used by most New England Indians were so thin that the dye soaked right through it.

Shopping bag made of Hong Kong grass and dark blue ash splints. 6" w, 13½" l, 9½" h. $37–$54

Jewelry Basket

The small jewelry and sewing baskets were interchangeable, but the ones most readily acceptable for jewelry were small and round with three feet. The square and oblong style that opened on top were also used.

Ash-splint and sweet-grass jewelry box. 5" dia, 4" o.h. $40–$64

Jicarilla Indians

The Jicarillas were part of the Apache tribe that lived in northern New Mexico. The Apaches were somewhat nomadic, probably because they were constantly searching for water and less arid lands. The Jicarillas lived in teepees in open country but built brush shelters when in the mountains. They practiced some agriculture, but they depended mostly on wild plants, seeds, and game. Unlike so many of the other Indians, they did not become skilled in weaving, nor did they make much pottery, but they did make fine baskets.

Many of their early baskets had little or no decoration. When they began to sell baskets to the white collectors, they added designs. Their work was exquisite, and it was said that as many as 100,000 stitches might be used in one large tray. The work was so intricate it might take a year to complete a large tray.

Finely coiled tray could have been made by the Jicarillas. $500–$700

Jigger-Glass Basket

The jigger-glass basket is generally a bit smaller than the medicine-glass basket; otherwise, they are almost identical, if made by the same makers or in the same area. These little baskets could be taken on picnics or on trips, because the basket protected the glass inside.

Ash-splint and sweet-grass jigger-glass basket. 2" dia, 2½" h. $21–$30

Judas Tree

Thought to be of European and Asiatic origin, this is supposed to be the kind of tree on which Judas hanged himself. Since the exact tree is not known, many varieties fall into this category, including the redbud. The redbud bears small, budlike pink flowers, and the young limbs are excellent for use in basketry.

Jugs and Demijohns, Basketry-Covered

The majority of the larger jugs and demijohns were used for shipping alcoholic beverages, particularly rum. Ships from New England sailed to South American ports where they traded their cargo of everything from lumber and ice for rum. Most of the rum was brought home in kegs and barrels, but a good amount was carried in jugs and demijohns. Fresh water for the long sea trips was also carried in the basketry-covered containers. The basketry covers protected the glass containers on the long trips. Incidentally, these jugs are fast becoming decorator items, and prices are rising rapidly.

Green glass jug totally encased in basketry. Gallon size. $25–$35

Amber demijohn, 2½-gallon size. $39–$55

Kaitel

The Indian name for the Hupa baby basket. See "Hupa Baby Basket" under "Baby-Related Basketry."

Kakisookbe

Kakisookbe is the old term the Penobscots used for ash splints. It meant the splints were very flexible and would not break easily, a necessary feature when making fancy designs on baskets. See "Wicopy."

Kettle Baskets

No explanation has been found for the practice of making baskets in the shape of old iron kettles. Somebody probably decided to copy the shape, and others followed suit.

Large kettle basket made of thicker ash splints. Different swing handle. Unity College collection. $85–$135

Small kettle basket made of ash splints and sweet grass. Unity College collection. $44–$75

Knee Vice

Basketmakers had to be ingenious to design their own baskets, and more ingenuity was needed to copy the designs of others and improve upon them. Even more was needed for basketmakers to devise and make tools that would fit their individual needs, tools that were easier to use, as well as tools that would make the work easier.

Some basketmakers built shaving horses, which are a bit more sophisticated than the plain knee vice or clamp. All of these tools were used to apply an even pressure to the annual layers of ash so it could be pulled apart. With the horse or the vices, the layers could be peeled in half lengthwise, over and over, until the splints were paper-thin. Some basketmakers got so skilled in this process that the splints they divided with these tools became satin smooth and looked as if they had been polished. That, of course, accounts for some of the lovely finishes on old baskets today.

The knee vice was placed between the knees where pressure was applied. $45–$79

The Mohawk name for this tool is *Teienanetakwatha.*

Some knee vices were made to sit on the floor, as opposed to being held between the knees. This means the sides are taller and have to be held together. On the one pictured a rope was used. These tools could be used for other chores requiring a vice, as well as for making splints.

116

Floor model knee vice. $65–$95

Knife Box, Basketry

There was a time when knives were kept in boxes, first in very elegant, upright boxes that sat on sideboards in formal dining rooms, and then in wooden knife boxes with han-

Late basketry knife box. 6" w, 11" l, 2¾" h. $25–$39

dles in the center. Later this knife box with the handle in the center would be copied in basketry. The basketry ones were very popular because they were lighter, cheaper, and easier to use. The glass spoon holder usually held both spoons and forks, so all that was needed were knives. Knives could be put into the knife box as soon as they were washed, and at mealtime taken to the table.

Knotted Carrying Baskets

It's not clear who made the first knotted (net) carrying baskets. The Indians made them using a variety of fibers, and the white sailors are known to have knotted everything from baskets to canopies for the bed. Knotted carrying baskets are no longer needed, but old sailors continue to knot small souvenir-type baskets.

New, small knotted carrying basket. 8" l. $5–$8

Koasati Indians

Another name for the Louisiana Coushattas. See "Coushatta Indians."

Kudzu Vine

Oriental *kudzu* was imported into the southern states for two reasons—to help stop soil erosion and feed livestock. It has served its purpose well in both areas. The fast-growing vine has been checked and measured to determine its overnight growth. Experts agree it will grow as much as 18 inches overnight. Even though this vine makes good cattle feed, it grows so quickly that the cattle can't keep it under control.

During the summer, the landscape in parts of the South is often a sea of green leaves as kudzu vines spread over the trees, utility poles, and anything else in its path. People who dislike kudzu, and there are plenty of them, have been unable to eradicate it. Therefore, there was rejoicing in Georgia when one of their own, Regina

Traditional basket made of split kudzu vine. 9½" w, 11" l, 15" o.h. $25–$45

Hines, began making baskets using kudzu vines. At first she made traditional baskets, but then she noticed that the vines grew in beautiful—if sometimes grotesque—shapes, so she began making free-form baskets.

The vines are gathered in early spring or late fall, while they are still reasonably green. Completely dried or dead vines are too brittle and will break as one works with them. Small vines can be used in the traditional baskets, or the large ones can be split. The bark, or outside, is left on the vines to give them an instant antique appearance. Hines has built a thriving basket business in Georgia; in fact, kudzu baskets became so popular, she now teaches a class at a local college.

Lamps

Boudoir

A picture of a boudoir lamp along with instructions for making it was given in a 1925 book on basketry. If the maker used the materials suggested, the base of the lamp would be 11 inches, the author said. The shade would be 7 inches in diameter and 9

Free-form kudzu basket. 11" dia, 16" o.h. $25–$40

inches tall. On this one the author suggested the use of lots of wooden beads in five different sizes.

Floor

Instructions were also given in the 1925 basketmaking book for floor lamps, and if the wooden beads had been left out, it would be difficult today to tell them from wicker floor lamps.

Information on bead use was included. Anyone using the wooden beads was warned to keep them dry, because if they were allowed to absorb water, they would crack later. It was also suggested that when the reeds were going to be dyed, perhaps to match the beads, the dyeing should be done before the work began. The beads took paint easily, the author said, and "any painted effect" could be worked out.

La Passiance

La passiance is a name given to the roots of the dock plant, any of several coarse weeds of the buckwheat family, used by the Chitimacha Indians to obtain the rich, bright red used in their cane baskets.

Laundry Baskets

The Pilgrims were not nearly as clean as the Victorians, who believed that "cleanliness was next to godliness" and proved it every Monday morning by washing everything that had been worn, been used, or looked dirty. The Victorians owned iron wash pots where clothing and linens were boiled in lye soap until whites were snow white and colored things were squeaky clean. They used laundry baskets to take the clothes to the pot and from the rinse to the clothes line.

Square, sturdy, oak-splint laundry basket. 22" sq, 10" h. $39–$50

Square, oak-splint laundry basket. 20" sq, 12" h. $65–$75

Lazy Squaw Weave

This was one of the first weaves described in the Navajo basket-weaving book published in 1903. The explanation was very interesting because it explained why the weaver would leave large spaces in the weave. In those days, the reed or rod was called a *bam*. It was said that if the squaw was lazy when making a basket, she would wrap the bam, or reed, two to four times before making the much harder stitch that was necessary to hold the reeds or bams together in the coiling of the foundation. The other squaws would criticize her and call her a lazy squaw; hence, the name for that stitch. This stitch does leave open spaces in an otherwise closely coiled basket.

Lids and Covers

The majority of the old splint baskets didn't have lids or covers in the beginning, and some of those that did have been lost through the years. On the other hand, Indian-made baskets, especially the fancy kind made in the Northeast, all seem to have had lids and covers. For most work and burden baskets, they really weren't necessary, but for the fancy ones, they were necessary and they made the baskets much prettier.

Making tops that would fit the baskets and boxes required more than ordinary skill. Actually, skill and experience, and maybe a little wizardry, were required to make lids for the small pine needle baskets—lids that must fit easily, yet firmly, in the inside of the small opening.

Lids were, and still are, made in several different shapes. The Coushatta Indians make lids with collars for their pine needle baskets. A *collared* lid is made with an inside collar that fits the lid perfectly inside the basket, regardless of its size or shape. The northeastern Indians also used collared lids, but many were flat, or they were lids with turned-down sides. Domed lids were made for the larger baskets.

The inside of a large ash-splint lid.

Lord, Albra

Lord was a basketmaker in Lovell, Maine, who made excellent baskets during the late 1800s and early 1900s. His baskets, especially the swing-handle ones, are very sought after by Mainers. Today, authentic Lord baskets bring exhorbitant prices. His baskets are round, with weavers that widen as they reach the top. The swing handles are fastened with copper rivets.

Swing-handle basket made by Albra Lord. 16" dia, 17" o.h. $500–$650

Lumbee Indians

Mystery surrounds the Lumbees. From the mid-1800s to the mid-1900s they were called Croatans. Speculation links them to the Lost Colony—the white settlers who vanished centuries ago—but no proof has been found to substantiate the theory. Then, there are those who believe the settlers intermarried with the Hatteras Indians and later migrated to the banks of the Lumber River in North Carolina. Due to their close association with white settlers, and their location in the Great Smoky mountain area, the Lumbee Indians have always made oak-splint baskets as well as vine baskets.

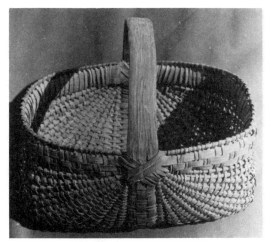

Same type splint basket as made by a Lumbee. $300–$495

Lunch Basket

The original use for the type of basket pictured is unknown. It may or may not have been designed to be a lunch basket, but during the Roaring Twenties such baskets were used by many children to take their lunches to school. It was ideal for the purpose. This one is made of rattan and cane and could

School lunch basket. 8½" w, 12" l, 12" o.h. $15–$23

have been made either in the States or in the Orient. School lunch baskets were made in a variety of styles and shapes by American basketmakers.

Mahogany Roots

Navajo Indians used the roots of the mahogany tree to make dye for the sumac they used to make baskets. Lumber from the trees might have been important to furniture makers, but the Indians of the southwest were only interested in the roots to make a reddish brown dye. The older Navajo women referred to it as "mountain mahogany."

Maidenhair Fern Stems

There are approximately 200 species of maidenhair fern. Only one, though, grows heartily in the North: American maidenhair. It is safe to assume that American maidenhair, or five-finger fern (pedatum), was the type of maidenhair fern used in the baskets made in America. Indian basketmakers used the stems more in their basketry than the whites. Generally, the fern stems were combined with spruce roots to make tightly woven or twined baskets.

Magazine Racks

Magazine racks were not made in a variety of styles until after the turn of the century. Before the twentieth century, there weren't many magazines being published. Magazines that were published weren't receiving much distribution. Thus, there wasn't a big demand for magazine racks, and basketmakers felt no compulsion to make them. They knew other baskets would sell, so why bother to make a new item with a questionable future? With the introduction of gas and steam heat, the need for the old woven firewood baskets decreased, and owners simply converted them to magazine racks. Not surprisingly, no instructions for magazine racks were found in the old basketry books.

Woven-splint magazine rack. 13" w, 18" l, 10" h.
$25–$49

Makah Indians

The Makahs have long been considered one of the more daring of the tribes living in the Northwest. Long before the arrival of the white man, they would go completely out of sight of land to search for whales. Since the whales were much larger than the boats, they would tow in the dead whale behind the little boat. They were so skilled in ocean travel, they could go out of sight of land and return, guided only by atmospheric conditions and the direction of the waves.

As in most Indian tribes, the women were the basketmakers, and shortly before the turn of the present century, they began making inexpensive, tourist-type baskets. They might have been inexpensive then, but they are very expensive now.

Being whaler families, they used that theme in many of their baskets. Their work is similar to other tribes in that area, especially the Nootka of British Columbia.

Most Makah baskets were made of cedar roots twined with bear grass, and they usually begin with a checkerwork bottom. The majority of the Makah baskets found today are twines, but they did, at an earlier time, make coiled baskets. Most of their baskets are lidded and are small, usually under 8 inches.

Small, open basket showing the checkerwork bottom. Made of cedar roots twined with bear grass. 2½" w, 4" l, 2½" h. $95–$150

Two whalers in boats are shown on either side of the small basket. Colors are red, green, and brown, and the boat is a kind of rust color. 2" dia, 2" h. $135–$225

Old Makah basket of cedar roots twined with grass. 3" dia, 1¾" h. $125–$200

Maliseet Indians

There are only about 2500 Maliseets living in Maine at the present time, but several centuries ago they were a powerful tribe, one to be reckoned with. They were semi-agricultural—they grew some corn, squash, and probably a few other things—but depended mainly on hunting and fishing for their food. Like so many other tribes of that era, they usually moved on a regular basis as they looked for better hunting and fishing grounds. Normally, the Maliseets resided near large bodies of water, as they were a seafaring people, and have been described as bold sailors who hunted seal, porpoise, and whale.

They were so closely associated with other Maine tribes (the Penobscots, Passamaquoddies, and Micmacs), and their work was so similar, it's difficult today for the average collector to differentiate between the baskets made by each tribe. Not only were the same basket materials available to all of them, they were also vying for the same tourist trade. Although they still won't admit it, they are believed to have "borrowed" ideas from one another and from the white basketmakers.

Older baskets, those 150 to 200 years

In Canada, for some reason this type basket, made of Hong Kong and sweet grass with ash splints, was called an arm basket. 10" dia, 6" h. **$43–$65**

Ash-splint and sweet-grass covered basket. 4" dia, 2½" h. **$18–$32**

Ash-splint basket typical of those made by the Maliseets. Unity College collection. **$48–$70**

This ash-splint basket was often called a carrying basket. 10" dia, 12" h. **$48–$60**

old, are not easy to find. For that reason, it's almost impossible to compare the earlier work of these tribes with their later basketry—the items made for the tourist trade. However, they did excellent work and apparently made thousands of baskets during their heyday.

Mallet

This tool is used like a hammer and is roughly the length of an ax. The handle is shaped to fit the hand while the 8- to 10-inch hammer-type head is left on the other end. The head is used to pound a wedge into oak trees to split them. The mallet is sometimes used to beat the ash so it will separate into the annual growth splints.

Market Baskets

It has been said that when the paper bag, the poke, and the cardboard carton replaced the handmade basket, we all became a little poorer.

At one time, the ladies living in cities, towns, and villages across the country took their beautiful handmade baskets over their arms each morning and sallied forth to buy food for the day. There was no way to preserve food other than canning or smoking; therefore, people chose the simpler and better way of buying fresh foods daily.

It is not unusual, now, to find old pictures showing a housewife going from one place to another with her market basket over her arm. There were no super markets and few general stores in those days. Instead, she shopped with independent merchants like the vegetable vendors, butchers, and those selling fresh fruits.

The style, shape, and design of the market basket might differ from one area to another, depending on the skills of the basketmaker and the preference of the housewife. Location also had a bearing on style and shape. Most market baskets were open, but occasionally covered ones can be found. It was easier for the shopper to drop her purchases in an open basket, and an

Oak-splint market basket from the mountain areas. 10" w, 12" l, 14" o.h. $175–$300

Larger-than-usual market basket. $125–$190

Oak-splint market basket. 13" w, 17" l, 16" o.h. $175–$225

124

Ash-splint market basket. 12" w, 14" l, 15" o.h.
$95–$115

Indian-made ash-splint market basket, reinforced rim. 12" w, 14" l, 15" o.h. $44–$85

Factory-made market basket, materials unknown. 12" w, 20" l, 14" o.h. $34–$49

open basket could hold more than a closed basket. Some market baskets were made stronger than ordinary baskets—food could be heavy to carry.

The market basket was also used for other shopping trips; there were no large shopping bags made of paper in the dry goods stores in those days. It was much easier to use the market basket or a smaller shopping basket than to try to keep up with numerous loose packages.

Marriage Basket

Long ago, baskets similar to the one pictured were used in the marriage of Seneca Indian girls. Such baskets might have been used by all the tribes of the Six Nations, but they were definitely used by the Senecas.

The mother of the bride would fill the marriage basket with corn bread and then take the bread-filled basket and her daughter to the home of the groom (and then leave). The girl would take her basket of bread into the family home of the groom, where she would live until she had a home of her own.

Basket similar to the marriage basket used by the Senecas. 13" dia, 12" h. $75–$135

Mats

Basketmakers skilled in basketry made other things using the basketry techniques of weaving, coiling, and twining. After the twisting, turning, and shaping of baskets, it must have been easy to make flat items like mats. Mats were necessary and were made by most of the Indians, especially those east of the Plains. Mats served a dual role—they could be used as decorative wall hangings, or they could be used as floor mats for the family to sit on when eating or visiting. Usually made of river or swamp cane, these mats were dyed the same as other basketry items. Few are made today, except those made to be sold in arts and crafts outlets.

Old Chitimacha cane mat with worn edges and center. $300–$500

Maul

Maul is another name for mallet. See "Mallet."

May Baskets

Until recently, it was customary for children and some adults to take small baskets of flowers to the sick and the shut-ins, or as an expression of appreciation to someone who had been kind to them.

It's believed the custom was a variation of the old English custom of "Going-a-Maying." It was customary during the sixteenth and seventeenth centuries for the middle and lower classes to go out early in the morning on the first day of May to gather flowers and hawthorn branches. The hawthorn blossom was named *May,* which accounts for the phrase "bringing home the May." Early in the morning they would go merrily into the woods and fields, accompanied by the music of a horn, and gather flowers and greenery. Around sunrise they would have enough to decorate all the doors and houses in the village and would return to the village to begin that task.

In earlier times, kings and queens attended these festivities, which probably accounted for their popularity then. May Day festivities became so famous, they were celebrated throughout the British Empire.

Medicine-Glass Basket

There isn't too much difference between medicine-glass baskets and jigger-glass baskets, other than size and the whims of the basketmaker. The sickroom looked better with a basketry-covered glass than with just a plain medicine glass.

These basketry items were another thing that could be made using scraps and left overs from larger baskets. Short pieces of ash-splint could be used to weave the sweet grass over. And there is a chance that the fragrance of the sweet grass took away some of the unpleasant odor of the medicine.

Ash-splint and sweet-grass medicine-glass basket. 2½" dia, 3" h. $23–$38

Melon Basket

So-called because of the shape; in fact, it is sometimes called a half-melon basket. Regardless of the name, it was a very popular basket in the mountain areas. There it was often used instead of the gizzard or buttocks basket for gathering eggs, storing eggs, and taking eggs to the store to sell. Melon baskets were always made of oak splints and were much more popular in the South than in the northern states. Workmanship was

usually excellent. Due to the scarcity, they are now rather expensive.

Mescalero Indians

The Mescaleros lived in teepees when they lived in open country, but they went back to brush shelters when in the mountains. They grew some vegetables and corn but depended mostly on wild plants, seeds, and game for food. They are said not to have been too interested nor too skilled in weaving fabric, nor were they involved in pottery as so many other tribes were. But reports are they made fine baskets—when they wanted to.

It is a fairly well-known fact that the Mescaleros were one of the tribes who more or less lost interest in basketmaking until the white traders arrived. With the arrival of these traders, who offered them all manner of barter items for their baskets, their interest was renewed, and they began making quality baskets that could be sold or traded easily.

The Mescaleros, part of the Apache tribe (along with some other tribes), used the coiled tray or basket in the girl's puberty rites, which would indicate that they continued to make some baskets through the years. Like so many others in the Southwest, they used the materials available to them. Usually a

White oak-splint melon basket. 7" w, 12" l, 11" h. $200–$300

Coiled tray with typical Mescalero design. 12" dia. $350–$600

basket's foundation was made of sumac stems, and the sewing was done with yucca. Decoration was done with devil's claw and colored yucca. For a larger burden basket, the foundation was of mulberry.

Miccosukee Indians

The Miccosukees acknowledge that their origin has been lost and now lives only in legends, but they're proud of being part of the Creek confederacy—a loosely organized group of Indians living along the rivers and creeks of Alabama, Georgia, and the Carolinas. The Miccosukees were neither nomadic nor warlike. They preferred to live, farm, hunt, and fish in the same area.

Materials used in making Miccosukee baskets with an almost-finished basket.

First few rows of a coiled basket on patchwork background.

Pine needle basket with colorful design (new). $130–$150

Pine needle basket with doll head finial. $90–$110

Early in the eighteenth century, a group known as the Mikasukis settled near what is now Tallahassee, Florida. The name soon took on the phonetic sound, *Miccosukee,* the name they are known by today. When the Miccosukee were to be sent to Oklahoma with other Indians, many of them hid in the Everglades and remained there in hiding until around 1870, when they began trading furs, plumes, and hides for supplies. The government soon passed laws prohibiting the sale of egret plumes and alligator hides, so they returned to their *chickees* in the Everglades.

A *chickee* is a house of sorts, or dwelling, designed and built by the Miccosukee in the Everglades, using available materials, to suit the hot, humid weather. A typical chickee is approximately 16 feet long by 9 feet wide and is built on a platform about 3 feet off the ground. The purpose of elevating the homes is, of course, to protect the people from floods, but also to protect them from snakes and other creatures of the Everglades. Cypress poles are used to support the roof, and smaller cypress poles are used to hold the cabbage palm or palmetto fronds that are used to cover the roof.

Although it upset the ecology of the Everglades somewhat, the building of the Tamiami Trail that connects Miami with the west coast of Florida was a blessing for the Miccosukee. It has brought hundreds of tourists past their doors—tourists who stop to buy the beautiful patchwork for which the Miccosukee are justly famous, as well as paintings, dolls, beadwork, wood carvings, and pine needle baskets.

Through the years, the Miccosukees have used many basket materials indigenous to the area, such as cane, cabbage palm stalks, grasses, fronds, strips of bark, and pine needles. But in recent years, most of their basketmaking for the tourist trade has been in pine needles. They use the coil technique, but with a difference—the base of the basket is made with a circle of strong cardboard covered on both sides with palmetto fiber. The coiling starts on the edge of the circle.

Another difference in their baskets is that instead of using raffia, as do other basketmakers when working with pine needles, they use brilliantly colored thread that's been pulled through beeswax to strengthen it. Like the raffia, the thread is used to make designs.

Micmac Indians

The first meeting between the Micmac Indians in Maine and the white settlers occurred on the coast near Cape Neddick in 1602. At that time, the Micmac called themselves *Ul'noo,* or *the people.* The corruption began with the term *nikmag,* which meant "kin-friend," an indication of their relationship with the whites. The nikmag name tag stuck and eventually became Micmac, despite the fact that the French orig-

Old ash-splint potato basket. $35–$50

Well-made ash-splint basket, Unity College collection. $150–$250

Covered ash-splint and sweet-grass box. 4" dia, 2½" h. $30–$49

Hong Kong grass and ash-splint box. 5½" dia, 3⅜" h. $29–$38

inally called them Souriquois and the English referred to them as Tarentines.

Today, the Micmacs are one of the largest tribes east of the Mississippi River. There are over 12,000 Micmacs in New England, with an additional 7000 in the Maritimes. About 900 Micmacs live in Maine, mostly in the potato-growing area of Aroostook County.

The Micmacs were long considered a migratory tribe who "followed the fish." They've always had their own language and culture, and they are skilled basketmakers.

Basketmaking was essential in the early days for migratory people, who did not have paper bags, boxes, or trunks. For that reason, they learned how to make heavy burden baskets as well as lightweight "moving" baskets. They also made any other containers one might need, including cooking and storage containers. Many of these were made of birch bark tied with spruce root. They made bags by weaving flat strips of the soft inner bark of cedar and basswood trees.

They used basswood in many ways. The strips of bark could be rolled into cords and later woven into baskets and mats. Oftentimes, they made twine of Indian hemp and used it with the bark of trees and with reeds. They made baskets of bark, roots, rush, and tough grasses, but today, they are probably better known for their ash-splint baskets—the finer ones made of paper-thin splints and

Sweet-grass and ash-splint container, opens in middle; Unity College collection. $35–$69

woven with sweet grass—and their porcupine quill baskets and boxes. To make porcupine quill boxes they had to pluck the quills from dead porcupines, dye them, and then insert them in a design in birch-bark boxes. They also made baskets and boxes entirely of birch bark and then scratched off part of the outer bark to make a design; or they painted a design.

The Micmacs still make potato-gathering baskets, but the demand is very low now that machinery is used for the gathering. It's difficult to attribute certain baskets to any one tribe, since the baskets are so similar among the many different tribes.

Milk Bottle Basket

Through the years, many wine and beverage bottlers, as well as individuals, have encased bottles in basketry. It's doubtful though, that too many people made a basket just to fit a one-quart milk bottle. The bottle basket shown here is believed to be one of a kind. It was made by a Penobscot Indian lady for her son's use when bringing home a quart of milk. Her son still remembers how he left the basket at the store in the

Ash-splint basket made to hold one-quart milk bottle. $75–$95

morning on his way to school and picked it and the milk up on his way home in the afternoon. Later, she made one to fit a half-gallon bottle or jug, but no one knows what happened to it.

Milkweed

Milkweed grows wild over much of the country. It has a milky juice; hence, the name. There are two species that work well in basketry: one is the white milkweed, the other is red milkweed. In basketry, the stems are beaten until they separate into silky fibers, and then they are twisted into two-strand cords that can be used like sweet grass for weaving baskets. When twisted, the cord becomes very tough, yet remains pliable. When red and white milkweed are twisted together, they make a beautiful red and white rope. Shredded milkweed also makes a soft foundation material for coiled baskets.

Mill Baskets

Baskets were used in Northern mills, but it is difficult to tell which type of basket was used in which type of mill—cotton, silk, or woolen. The two baskets shown here were used in different mills, or at least for different chores. Oldtimers say these baskets were used in mills to transport various materials like thread, yarn, and finished fabric from one department to another. They are almost as large as the old balloon baskets, but are more closely woven. Made of willow, mill baskets are really too large to be collectible, except for nostalgic purposes.

Two mill baskets. $25–$40

Miniature Baskets

Making miniature baskets seems to intrigue old basketmakers as much as making novelties and oddities. They make miniature baskets using many different materials. The variety of miniature baskets includes a tiny Indian-made bead basket measuring only one-half inch in diameter to less than one inch in height. The Choctaws make a cane basket with a lovely dyed design that measures 1½ inches in diameter and 3 inches in

An oak-splint basket shown next to a quarter to indicate its size. $250–$400

Finely woven miniature oak-splint baskets: (left) 1½" dia, 2" h, $200–$300; (right) 2" dia, 3" h, $250–$475.

Ten-year-old miniature basket. 3¼" dia, 4" o.h. $15–$20

New miniature herb basket. 3½" w, 5" h, $5–$7

Basketry-covered bottle. 1" dia bottom, 4" h. $5–$8

Rattan minnow basket. Base 6½" dia, top 3½" dia, 4½" h, minnow opening 1" dia. $25–$40

Like everything else in basketry, minnow baskets were made in a variety of sizes, to fit the needs of the person using them. The top of the basket pictured is missing, but likely it was covered with either screen wire or mosquito netting and tied in place with the four strings attached to the bottom of the basket.

Miscellaneous Baskets

This category includes baskets still being researched. In some cases, the materials used to make them are known; for others, only the use or what is believed to have been the use of the basket is known. The baskets pictured are included here to show the types of baskets being offered today in antique shops, shows, and malls.

Ash-splint basket, use unknown; Unity College collection. $35–$50

height. Both the Cherokees and the Indians of the Northeast make sweet-grass and splint baskets just as small. They take great pride in making tiny baskets with tiny stitches. In fact, 40 stitches per inch is average on some of their small baskets, and some even have as fine as 60 to 70 stitches per inch.

Minnow Baskets

When our ancestors were going down to the creek to catch a few fish for supper, it never occurred to them to buy minnows or bait. They simply put the minnow basket in the shallow side of the creek or branch and caught enough minnows for that fishing trip.

Open-weave bottom with sweet-grass flange, use unknown; Unity college collection. $30–$49

Two similar baskets made of vine; probably fruit baskets. White, 11" dia, 6" h; natural 10" w, 13" l, 5" h. $15–$25 ea.

Oak-splint basket, use unknown. 18" dia, 13" h. $75–$135

Factory-made oak-splint basket, use unknown. 20° sq, 15" h. $30–$40

Square, brightly colored, ash-splint-covered basket, use unknown; Unity College collection. $77–$99

Factory-made oak-splint basket, use unknown, 12" square, 15" o.h. $45–$50

Colorful twined mat believed to have been made by one of the western Indian tribes. $150–$250

Vine wastebasket; appears to be Oriental. 11½" dia, 7¼" h. $15–$20

Small ash-splint basket painted dark red on the ends and sides; the rest is natural. Could have been some type of harvesting basket or a small laundry basket. 12½" w, 19" l, 7½" h. $48–$72

Colorful oblong woven tray, appears to be made of some type of heavy fiber, use unknown. 6" w, 20" l, 4" h. $18–$33

Mission Indians

In the early days, the Mission Indians were prolific basketmakers. Their materials (which were mostly sumac and rush) and their weaves were limited. The Mission Indians' baskets were influenced by the Franciscan friars who controlled the missions of California. Friars supplied them with manufactured utensils, eliminating the need for much basketmaking.

Work similar to that by Mission Indians, 11¼″ dia, 5½″ h. $95–$175

In the early days, their work may have been of better quality, but in later years they used a coarser construction, with four to eight stitches per inch considered common.

Mohawk Indians

The Mohawks were part of the powerful Five Nations (comprised of Oneidas, Onandagas, Cayugas, Mohawks, and Senecas) that controlled most of what is now northern New York, southern Ontario, portions of Pennsylvania, and Ohio.

During the eighteenth century, the Tuscaroras joined this group to form Six Nations, making it even more powerful. The Six Nations became so powerful and so well organized, they were apt to declare war on anyone who threatened their territory.

The Mohawks were less nomadic than most tribes. They settled into houses—well-built houses with gabled roofs—and they were farming people. They had large, well-tended cornfields and larger-than-average vegetable gardens. For meat, they depended on hunting and fishing and were very skilled with their long, flat bows and bone fishhooks.

Since they stayed in one area, they could have more household utensils. They had items like wooden bowls, trays, spoons, and mortars and pestles, and they had an abundance of fine baskets.

Drum purse believed to have been made by the Mohawks. 8″ dia, 3″ h. $65–$95

Top of covered ash-splint and sweet-grass basket, braided frog handle. 10″ dia, 4″ h. $38–$72

Baskets found today, and known to have been made by Mohawks, are usually the tourist type, very similar to those made by New England tribes. They also used ash splints and sweet grass for most of their baskets. Some of the older Mohawk baskets are darker than those known to have been made in New England, but this could stem from the fact they used the heart of the ash, which is naturally darker.

Unless the provenance is known, it's easy to assign baskets made by one tribe to another (incorrect) tribe.

Moose-Hair Embroidery

Moose-hair embroidery, like so many other tedious chores of the past, seems to be a lost art form. In 15 years of searching, this author has found only one moose-hair-embroidered piece. The one shown here is the only one in the over 500-item Terry collection at Unity College, Unity, Maine. The late Mr. Terry studied and taught Indian culture and collected Indian-made baskets for years, but he found only one embroidered with moose hair (pictured). Perhaps the task was so tedious and time-consuming that it was not practiced on a large scale.

In 1932, writing about the art of moose-hair embroidery in her book, *The Handicrafts of the Modern Indians of Maine*, Fannie Hardy Eckstorm said she was convinced that the work was done by the Huron Indians of Canada, as opposed to the Penobscots. She based her theory on the fact that her father had a large trading post at Old Town, Maine, during the 1870s, where he employed Penobscots to tan moose hides and then cut moccasins from them. Eckstorm's father left records stating that in 1872 he hired a Huron Indian who was visiting Old Town to help with the tanning and cutting. The Huron saved the long white hair he found on the throats of the winter-killed moose. He saved the white hair but returned the brown hair that was shaved off the moose hides. At that time, brown moose hair sold for around 10 cents a pound in Maine, while the long white hairs brought as much as 2 dollars a pound in Quebec, where it was used for moose-hair embroidery.

As soon as Eckstorm's father learned that the Canadian Hurons were skilled in

Ash-splint yarn basket with two rows of Hong Kong grass, bottom and top; wide splints. 6½" dia, 10" h. $30–$40

Squatty yarn basket, ash splint and Hong Kong grass. 7" dia, 6½" h. $43–$60

Small, round birch-bark box with moose-hair embroidery. Terry Collection, Unity College, $200–$250

Morita Skintaro

Morita Skintaro was a Kyoto basketmaker who gained quite a reputation for his bamboo baskets. One of the secrets of his fine basketry was the fact he lived in an area that grew some of the finest, tallest, and straightest bamboo.

Mulberry

The mulberry tree served dual roles in American life. The flexible branches and shoots have long been recognized as good basketry material; like willow branches, those from the mulberry can be split to make fine weavers. The leaves were used as food for silkworms.

Mystery Basket

Even the most advanced collectors occasionally find something that defies rhyme and reason. That was the case with the basket we have elected to designate a "mystery basket." There isn't a problem with the basket, itself—it's a coiled, Indian-made basket approximately a hundred years old. The mystery evolved when the basket was opened and there, among the yellowed tissues, was a paper-thin, porcelain-covered cup and saucer believed to be a rice cup. Judging by the way it fit into the tissues and basket, the china must have been in the basket for a long time. The question is: How did the china and the basket get together? Perhaps years

moose-hair embroidery, he sent the long white moose hair and the cut-out moccasins to them to be embroidered. When they were returned, the Penobscots sewed them together.

It's nearly impossible to imagine how the beautiful embroidery was accomplished with only long hairs from the neck of a moose, but it is exquisite. Some of the hairs were dyed in brilliant hues of green, red, yellow, and purple and were used with the white to make designs—floral designs in the case of the box pictured.

Mori-Kago

The Japanese name for a gift fruit basket is *mori-kago*. There was a time when gift giving flourished in Japan, and one of the most popular gifts was a basket of fresh fruit. As usual, the Japanese were concerned with the appearance of their gifts and made baskets best suited for the types of fruit each basket would contain. Oftentimes, the baskets were more valuable than the fruit.

Yucca-wrapped rush-covered basket with china. $6\frac{1}{2}$" dia, $3\frac{3}{4}$" h. $49–$78

ago someone put the china in the basket and gave it as a gift. The recipient apparently had never used it and, instead, had packed it away and forgotten about it.

Nantucket Lightship Baskets

The making of the woven basket that would become known as the *Nantucket Lightship basket* began around 1850. The majority of these baskets were either round or oval in shape, with wooden bases and movable handles attached to a pair of ears. They were often made in sets of seven or eight, and those sets have become extremely scarce and expensive (the old ones, that is). They are still being copied, and even the new ones are commanding high prices.

The Nantucket area had long been famous for whaling, but with the discovery of petroleum and kerosene, whale oil was no longer essential. Thus, whaling became much less important.

Rather than trying to build a much-needed lighthouse, an impossible task, it

seemed, at the time, the sailors of Nantucket anchored a lightship off the shore of the tiny Nantucket Island in Massachusetts. Several sailors were always on board to keep the light burning. Tours of duty on the lightship were usually eight months long, so the sailors began making baskets to avoid the boredom—and they developed their own style.

The baskets became so popular, they began to be copied shortly after the first ones were shown. Differentiating between

In Spring 1989, this Nantucket basket sold for $1050 at a Maine auction.

Well-made Nantucket basket. 15" dia, 16" o.h. $715–$900

Nest of three small Nantucket baskets. $2500–$3500

those actually made by the sailors and those made by basketmakers in the area requires an expert. Those made by the lightship sailors (up until around 1895) and those made by others, including some of the retired sailors, are now selling at five-figure prices when found in well-preserved nested sets.

The demand for this type of basket has been persistent and remains so, even today. Several modern basketmakers continue to make Nantucket Lightship-style baskets. A set of seven new nested baskets copied after the Nantucket lightship style, sold at a Maine auction, in 1988, for $4500. New ones can be found all over New England, and most are sold as single baskets, rather than nested, with prices ranging from $200 to $300 for the smaller sizes, up to $500 or more for the larger ones.

Whether or not handleless Nantucket baskets were made aboard the lightship or by people in the area who copied the work of the sailors is not known. The handleless basket pictured is old, and the workmanship beautiful. Very few have been seen without handles.

Nantucket Lightship–Type Purses

Around 1940, a Filipino decided to copy the old Nantucket baskets, making a smaller version. He added a top and made a lady's purse. The basket-purses became an instant success—so much so, in fact, that others began to copy the style. At first, these baskets were considered a fad or a novelty, but during the past few years they have become very collectible.

The Nantucket Lightship-type purse has a wooden base, like the baskets, and the lid has a small wooden disc, usually with some kind of decoration on it. Often the decoration is a carved fish or bird or a handpainted design. Many will have the name or initials of the maker. Older ones are now showing up in antique shops, shows, and malls in New England, with prices ranging from $95,

Nantucket-type basket without handles. 15" dia, 4" h. $300–$450

Inside of same basket.

Early Nantucket-type basket-purse with the maker's name handpainted on the disc. $150–$300

for less-than-perfect examples, to as much as $300 for perfect ones. In other areas they may be priced higher. In fact, some contemporary basketmakers are now making their own versions of the basket purses; finer examples are priced in the $500 range.

Napkin Rings

The Victorian housewife was as fussy about her household linens as the Colonials were about their feather and down beds. There were few places to entertain guests outside the home, so she took great pride in snowy white tablecloths and napkins, which were

Another type of sweet-grass napkin ring. Unity College collection. $6–$10

Sweet-grass napkin ring with ash-splint bow. $5–$9

Porcupine quills have been inserted into a birch-bark napkin ring leaving the bark border. 2" dia, 1½" h. Single ring, $15–$25; set of six, $95–$150

always ironed to perfection. The napkins could be placed in a folded position on the table, folded into an ornate shape, or rolled and placed in napkin rings. Napkin rings were made in silver, cut glass, ivory, and heaven knows what other materials, but the ones of more interest to basket collectors are the ones made of cane and grasses.

Cane napkin rings could have been made by southern basketmakers who had access to cane. There is little doubt that most of the sweet-grass napkin rings were made by basketmakers of the Northeast.

Navajo Basket-Weaving Book

Indian Basket Weaving was published by the Navajo School of Indian Basketry in 1903. It contained about 100 pages of instructions for making baskets exactly as the Indians made them, along with photos of fine old Indian-made baskets. At least 20 different weaves were explained in simple enough detail that anyone could follow the instructions. Information was given on various materials, as well as all the necessary instructions on sizes and splicing.

The book was advertised in women's magazines. By following its instructions, a person could make replicas of baskets made by the western Indians. Apparently, a great number of baskets were made; they are now

141

appearing in antique shops, shows, and malls, and are labeled "Indian baskets."

Purists will argue that these baskets were made only according to western Indian designs, but those searching desperately for an example of these old baskets made *after* the western-Indian style welcome the chance to buy them for one tenth the price of the original. The baskets are well made; colorful, but faded; and old. Most appear to have been made of vine or rush, tightly woven with raffia.

Two baskets made by Navajo instruction-book directions: (left) 10″ dia, 3½″ h, $60–$90; (right) 8″ dia, 2½″ h, $55–$85

Covered basket made according to Navajo instructions. 10″ dia, 4″ h. $85–$115

Colorful basket according to Navajo instructions. 10″ dia, 3″ h. $69–$75

Navajo Indians

The Navajos (along with the Apaches) began moving southward from Canada around the thirteenth century. They always moved southwesterly, heading for Arizona. Their name, also spelled *Havaho,* means "large cultivated fields." They called themselves *Dine* (pronounced *dih-NAY*), meaning "the people." Today, they're one of the largest tribes in the States, with approximately 160,000 members. About 110,000 live on the 16-million acre reservation in Arizona.

Baskets have been a part of the Navajo culture for so long, they're even mentioned in the Navajo Origin myth. According to that myth, the men and women at one time began considering living separate lives. Before they could do that, however, the man had to consider whether or not he could handle the woman's chores such as cooking, making pottery, and most important, making baskets.

From the very beginning, the Navajos made burden baskets, water jugs, and other types of baskets, including the famous wedding basket. Generally, their baskets were made with a twined weave, using a three-rod foundation woven with sumac.

Baskets were always essential to Navajo tribal ceremonies, but no other type of basket was used more than the wedding basket. It was, and still is, used for serving cornmeal mush at weddings and as a recepticle for sacred items, and it was sometimes used as a drum.

Gathering sumac for the Navajo baskets was similar to gathering cane for baskets made by the Chocktaws and Cherokees. They first went to the fields where sumac grew and crawled around among the sumac bushes to find just the right kinds of branches. Then, once the branches were taken home, the Navajos tore them apart with their hands and teeth, much like the process used on cane. Sumac branches came apart in three pieces and were allowed to dry thoroughly before being rubbed with buckskin to remove the parts not needed in the basketry.

Only three colors were ever used to make the Navajo wedding baskets: red, white, and black. Roots of mountain mahaghony were used to make red dye. Once the sumac had been cleaned and dyed, it was time to begin making the basket.

It took patience and endurance to make a Navajo wedding basket, and only experienced basketmakers were allowed to make wedding baskets. (It took about three years to become experienced.)

Old Navajo wedding basket. Terry Collection, Unity College. $750–$1000

New Navajo wedding basket. 13" dia. $200–$300

After the white man came, the Navajos began using more metal containers, and so basket production slowed considerably. They continued to make baskets—a craft they continue today—but they were not as dependent on baskets after the white man came.

Then, restrictions were imposed on the Navajos making baskets—restrictions so complicated, many Navajo women stopped making them altogether. In fact, production decreased so badly between the 1920s and 1950s, the Navajos were forced to buy some of their baskets from Ute and Paiute basketmakers. This helps to explain the scarcity of old Navajo baskets.

This situation has changed considerably in recent years. One reason for this is the demand for baskets, new or old; with that demand has come better prices—prices high enough to encourage Navajo women to resume basketmaking.

Navaho Indians

Another spelling for Navajo. See ''Navajo Indians.''

143

Necklaces

Bead Basket

Not all basketmakers do beading, but usually someone in a basketmaking family does, making it easy to obtain baskets of beads as well as splints. They use the same type beads as they used on clothing and moccasins. These small baskets made of beads make interesting necklaces when used on a

Miniature basket necklace. $\frac{3}{4}$" dia, 1" o.h. $45–$60 on gold plated chain.

gold or silver chain. The tiny ones can be used to make earrings.

Coiled Horsehair

Indians in the Southwest have long made small baskets out of horsehair, but horsehair necklaces are rare. Twelve small discs, ranging in size from $\frac{7}{8}$ of an inch to 1 inch in diameter and made of white horsehair wrapped with black horsehair, form the decoration on this black necklace, also of horsehair.

Woven Basket

Any of the miniature baskets will make an exquisite necklace when placed on a gold or silver chain. This one which measures a little over $\frac{3}{4}$ inches in diameter was made years ago by the Cherokees. It was made of fine oak splint and honeysuckle vine dyed with butternut.

Neglige or Negligee Basket

If you should happen to find a basket lined with fancy fabric and edged with frilly lace, you could have a *neglige basket,* as they were called in 1875. Directions were given for making them in a book published at that time. Chances are the lining fabric and lace has long since deteriorated, although the basket may still be good.

There is always the chance that somebody will find one and not recognize it, therefore a description is being given to help with identification. The book suggested that

Blue and white bead basket on sterling chain. $\frac{1}{2}$" dia, 1" o.h. $20–$30 including chain.

Coiled horsehair necklace. $125–$150

a 54-inch-long willow basket be used. A thin layer of cotton batting was placed inside and outside the basket, then covered with a lining. Sprigged Swiss muslin was sewn over the lining. Satin ribbon was run through a yard of lace insertion that was then sewn over all the seams in the muslin. Pockets of colored muslin lined with stiff crinoline with puffed covers of sprigged Swiss muslin were then sewn around the sides and ends of the basket. More lace and ribbon was used on the pockets. Two flounces, or ruffles, covered with appliqué, lace, or embroidery, were placed around the basket, while ribbon-covered rings formed the handles on either end.

Nested Baskets

Although numbers of baskets were made in nests of five or six and continue to be made occasionally by contemporary basketmakers, nevertheless a set of eight is a bit unusual. An inexperienced basketmaker apparently made this set, because they are so tightly fitted it didn't seem feasible to try to take them apart to photograph them. The workmanship is quite good and the decorative handles attractive, but they aren't very serviceable since it is next to impossible to separate them. They were made of ash splints and are approximately 50 to 75 years old. They are quite small considering they are a nest of eight.

Nest of eight tightly fitted baskets. Largest, 10" w, 16" l, 9" o.h. **$300–$400**

New Hampshire Baskets

Where and how the name *New Hampshire* became attached to this type basket remains a mystery, but it is surprising how many

New Hampshire basket with wooden reinforcements. 16" dia, 19" o.h. **$400–$660**

Base of basket.

145

New Hampshire basket with metal reinforcement. 14" dia, 18½" o.h. Band around top and handle made of ½"-thick splints. $250–$400

Close-up of base.

people use the name. More research is needed. In fact, the name Ben Higgins comes up now and then when these baskets are found. Some want to attribute the kind with the metal reinforcements to him while others say he made the ones with the wooden reinforcements.

Both baskets have woven bottoms, but there the difference ends, as one has metal reinforcements that are worked into the basket itself near the bottom, while the other has wooden splints that go almost halfway up the side before they are woven into the basket.

It would appear that two or more basketmakers were involved in making these baskets, although the makers aren't presently known. These baskets are becoming quite sought after, and prices are rising. In fact, the wooden reinforced one sold at auction for $660.

Nootka Indians

Although they live in British Columbia, the Nootkas have always been closely associated with the Makahs—probably due to the fact both are experienced whalers and work in the same area. The baskets made by the two tribes are so similar, it is almost impossible to distinguish between them. Collectors seldom try; they simply lump them together.

Nootka basket, $150–$300

Novelties in Basketry

Many of the small items like miniature baskets and animal effigies could be classed as novelties, but they fit better in their individual categories.

Oak Splints

There are 22 different species of the oak tree in this country, and probably only a few of them are excellent for making splints for baskets. Most people would describe oak splints as "made of white oak." The people living in the mountains, both the Great Smoky and the Ozarks, prefer white oak, and they use it extensively. It works up easily, makes a beautiful basket, and, judging by the number still available, is one of the more durable splints. Oak splints can be cut very fine or can be left wide and thick to make burden baskets.

Half-bushel oak-splint basket. $78–$100

Very popular oak-splint gizzard or buttocks basket. 12" dia, 14" o.h. $400–$700

Small, sturdy oak-splint basket. $30–$50

Two old oak-splint baskets made in the Great Smoky mountains. Large, $90–$125; small, $55–$90

Round oak-splint basket. 16" dia, 22" o.h. $200–$300

Small oak-splint basket. 10" dia, 11" h. $55–$80

Oak-splint basket filled with apples. 12" dia, 12" h. $77–$98

Obijwa Indians

Obijwa is the original name for the tribe now known as Chippewa. First settlers corrupted the name. See "Chippewa Indians."

Ogawa Hihei

Ogawa Hihei was a Japanese basketmaker who lived and worked in Osaka. His work was as famous and sought after in Japan as the work of some of the better basketmakers in America.

Oienteteienonnarhitawa

This is the Mohawk name for the gauge used to split ash splints into uniform widths. The gauges could be made to split the ash into strips that varied from $\frac{1}{16}$ of an inch to $1\frac{1}{4}$ inches. Like everything else in basketry, the gauges were made to fit each worker's needs. One of the gauges made by the Mohawks was of wood, with blades that cut from 15 to 20 strips at one time. See "Gauge, Hand-Held."

"Old" Paint on a New Basket

Antiques from New England that have retained some of the old paint—the old blue, red, gray, green, or mustard—will bring twice as much as those without paint (this is typical of country antiques). But there is a distinct difference between the old paint used long ago and the paint used more recently, no matter how adept some get at mixing paint that looks like the very old.

Ash-splint basket painted with "new" old blue. 8" dia, 7" h, 12" o.h. $20–$75 depending on location.

Antique baskets have become extremely popular (and expensive) during the past 15 to 20 years, and there are people who have tried to cash in on this growing market. They either make or buy new baskets and then paint them to disguise the newness. Some are getting very good at mixing colors that closely resemble the old ones.

The basket in the photograph is an example. The basket is very attractive, and the color isn't bad. After a few more years of wear it probably will be able to pass for old. It has a swing handle, a very attractive shape, and good workmanship.

Oneida Indians

It isn't often one finds some history included with a basket, but the embroidered piece pictured had a yellowed piece of paper inside, and in a scratchy scrawl reminiscent of that of Victorian ladies was written: "Very old. Oscar bought it from Oneida Indians when he was a boy in school in Lockport, New York." It is a birch-bark box with moose-hair embroidery.

Whether the lady just wanted to leave a record or whether the note was left for a friend or relative is not known, but notes like this are very helpful. This one suggests that the Oneidas as well as the Hurons made exquisite pieces. Other tribes also made some pieces like this one, but examples are scarce.

This piece would indicate that moose-hair embroidery was done by other tribes in the Iroquois family. Six tribes, Senecas, Onondagas, Cayugas, Mohawks, Tuscaroras, and Oneidas, made up the Six Nations. Naturally, they would share skills and ideas.

The design on this piece is unusual, as

Moose-hair-embroidered case. 5" h, 1" w, 2½" l. $125–$200

Reverse side of case.

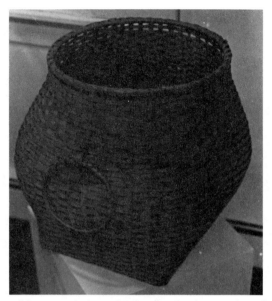

Old, unusual-shaped ash-splint basket attributed to the Penobscots; Unity College collection. $120–$195

most have floral designs. This one depicts an Indian smoking his peace pipe with trees in the background. The other side shows what was once a very colorful bird with a teepee on the lid.

Open Baskets

The style of basket and whether or not it had a lid depended, in part, on how it would be used. Most egg and market baskets were left open, since they were used daily by the owner. If the basket was going to be used as a picnic or lunch basket, it generally had a lid.

Baskets that were to be used for storage had covers to keep out mice, squirrels, and anything else that might eat the food and grain stored in the basket. Mice and squirrels could eat their way through thin splints, so basketmakers soon devised a way to combat the problem—they used thicker splints, and, in some cases, owners would tie the baskets to the ceiling.

Old Cherokee cane basket. $150–$225

Old swamp-cane basket attributed to the Choctaws. 12" w, 18" l, 13" o.h. $105–$200

Oriental Baskets

Although Oriental baskets are as old and as well made as other baskets, they've never sold for prices like other baskets. Recently, however, demand and price for these baskets have been increasing. Reasons for the Oriental basket's previous lack of popularity could be the influx of cheap baskets into this country before World War II and, more recently, the number of new baskets coming in from China and the Philippines.

A reason for the increasing popularity could be that many displaced Vietnamese are now making baskets, and since we realize that they make baskets by hand, just as our ancestors did, their baskets are more desirable.

Some of the older Oriental baskets were considered cheap and were sold in dime stores, and yet the opposite was often true—some were of excellent quality and workmanship.

As early as the turn of the twentieth century, some people were trying to interest collectors in the beauty of Oriental baske-

This is believed to be an old, willow Oriental purse. $45–$55

Bamboo wastebasket of the 1920s with a painted design around the sides. 12" dia, 13" h. $15–$29

Oriental basket often used as a sewing basket. Bamboo strips dyed vivid colors, no fading. 11" dia, 12" o.h. $18–$32

Bamboo basket with paper umbrella. 12" square, 12" o.h. $20–$39

Late bamboo wastebasket; note the bamboo-stalk legs. 16" dia, 14" h. $25–$35

try. One writer wrote that Oriental baskets were excellent examples of workmanship and were very artistically made. They were made as "objects of utility rather than as works of art," he wrote, "but the artistic element was introduced as the work progressed."

Oriental baskets, like teakwood furni-

ture, were made more elaborate for the American market, which is what the Oriental basketmakers believed we wanted.

The majority of Oriental basketry was made of bamboo, although various vines, rattan, and willow were also used. Bamboo and other materials were used to make handbags, cigar and cigarette cases, tobacco pouches, lunch boxes, sewing baskets, all types of fruit and flower baskets, and, later, wastebaskets.

Ose Basket

Another name for the broody hen basket. *Ose* refers to the material, willow, used to make the baskets. See "Hen Basket."

Ox Muzzles

Chances are good that woven muzzles were used more on calves than on grown oxen. Muzzles were used to keep young calves from nursing their mothers for too long; in other words, muzzles were used to wean them. Plow horses and oxen were muzzled to keep them from nibbling on crops—particularly young corn. Most muzzles resembled the horse-feeding basket but were made

Old, splint-woven ox muzzle. $135–$175

with loosely woven bottoms—if the animal had to wear them for long periods of time, this design allowed them to breath the fresh air more easily than did a regular horse-feeding basket.

Painted Baskets

Since baskets have become so popular as decorative accessories, and prices have spiraled accordingly, many ingenious people have begun buying and painting the old, cheap, factory-made baskets. Some are simply painted in bright colors, while others have designs added. A long time ago, this ordinary basket (below) was painted a rich green, and then a gold-leaf design of leaves and vines was added. Red dots were placed here and there to make it look like holly for a Christmas basket.

Factory-made basket painted and decorated. 6" w, 18" l, 10" o.h. $9–$20

Paint Removal

Some of the older basketmakers or basket owners painted their baskets. The painting of baskets was not common, but from time to time a basket will be seen in old paint, usually in one of the colors that were used on old pantry boxes.

During the Depression years, women painted many things to make them look fresh, including old baskets that were losing their usefulness because of the advent of new types of containers. With the paint the baskets were given a new identity and were given a

Goose basket that has had paint stripped off.

new place in the home. At that time money was scarce, so rather than trying to buy new things, people simply painted the old.

The paint on many of those old baskets can be removed by the new paint-stripping methods. In fact, the goose basket in the photograph was stripped by Amity Furniture Stripping, Westbrook, Maine, for a very modest price. The process doesn't seem to have had any harmful effects on the splints.

Not all baskets can be stripped. Those with fine splints seem to resist the process most.

Paiute Indians

The Paiute Indians have long been famous for their basketry. They have made some of

153

New Paiute tray in red and natural. 11" dia. $90–$175

Palm Leaves

Palm leaves were used to make the clutch purse shown here. This type of purse was made in Hawaii before World War II, and possibly afterward as well. It's made of coconut palm fronds in a checkerboard design. Palm leaves were also used to make hats, fans, and other woven items during that time. They were made in Florida and Cuba, as well as in South Carolina.

Clutch purse c. 1940, made of palm leaves. 9½" w, 13" l. $7–$14

the finest baskets available, including their beaded baskets. Unlike some of the western Indians, who would sew and weave bead designs into their baskets, the Paiutes would fasten their bead designs on the basket's top.

The Paiutes are part of the Shoshone group that is also famous for fine basketry. Most Paiute baskets were made in four colors—black, brown, red, and yellow.

Palmetto

Several species of palms growing in the southeastern part of the United States are lumped under the name *palmetto,* but only the Afro-American or Gullah people of the Low Country of South Carolina know the best ones to gather for their baskets.

All of the palms have served the people well. The wood of the cabbage palm is valued for its hardness and durability; the leaves of this palm, as well as those of other palm trees, are used to make hats, fans, and lacings for Gullah baskets.

The Afro-Americans gather the palmetto and place it in water for a short time. Then, after the palmetto is cut or torn into strips, they put it in the freezer for several weeks, which they say makes it work easier and better, and look better.

Papago Indians

The Papagos are close relatives of the Pimas. Because of their need to find water, they can be described as seminomadic.

The men did the farming while the women gathered cactus fruit, mesquite beans, and other wild-growing foods to supplement their meager harvest. If there wasn't enough rain to produce the crops they needed, they moved on.

Papago is a Pima word meaning "bean people," and it was acquired from their dependence on beans—cultivated beans when they could get them, mesquite beans when they could not.

The Papagos are still making baskets

New Papago basket, Yucca and devil's claw. 10"
dia. $75–$150

just as they have been for centuries, but today the newly made baskets are grabbed up by collectors rather than used by the Indians. The Papagos still use the same methods and materials: yucca and devil's claw. Old Papago baskets can be found from time to time, but they aren't plentiful.

Paper Rope Basketry

A paper rope basket immediately conjures up visions of Oriental baskets, probably paper rice baskets. But paper baskets were made in this country by women who became involved in the basketry revival of the 1920s.

Basket with cane spokes, paper weavers, and a
twisted vine handle. 7" w, 9½" l, 8" h. $12–$20

It was around 1920 that Dennison Manufacturing Company published a 32-page booklet of instructions for making all types of paper and wire baskets, trays, and even lamp shades.

To make the spokes, crepe paper was twisted around small wires. More crepe paper was twisted into ropes for weavers. The booklet listed a dozen different weaves, including Japanese single weave, pineapple, and arrowhead triple weave. Directions were given for making all types of baskets, including a heart-shaped basket and a sandwich basket. It also included directions for making a lamp base to be used with the paper rope shade. Any of the instructions could have been converted to use with other materials.

Party Baskets

During the Roaring Twenties, when a little girl had a birthday party, one thing was expected by the guests: fancy, crepe-paper baskets filled with nuts and mints. The crepe-

Crepe-paper party basket. 1½" w, 2¼" l, 4" o.h.
$5–$7

155

paper covered a lightweight cardboard base with a twisted paper handle topped by a paper flower. Sizes of the baskets ranged from 1½-by-2 inches up to twice that size. The color of the basket matched the color scheme of the party, which was usually pink. The smaller baskets could be bought for a few cents, while the larger, fancier ones could cost as much as five cents.

Pea Basket

In the Deep South where field peas and black-eyed peas grow in profusion, an oak-splint basket known as a *pea basket* was once used. These were made in assorted sizes—apparently to fit the needs of the picker. Although similar baskets were made and used in other areas, and were called by other names, the Southern pea basket was known for its taller handle, allowing the basket to be carried on the arm while leaving enough room for peas to be placed inside with no effort. The sides of the basket had to be just right—low enough to allow the peas to be put inside with little

Factory-made pea-picking basket. 12" w, 20" l, 2½" h. $35–$47

or no effort, yet high enough that the peas wouldn't fall out when the picker bent over to pick more.

Peat Basket

Long ago in Europe, peat, a partially decayed, moisture-absorbing plant matter found in old peat bogs and swamps, was used as fuel for heating homes. The peat had to be dug and then carried to the house—in a basket. The baskets were made large enough to accommodate quite a bit of peat, enough to keep the home fires burning for a while. The baskets were also used to bring in driftwood and dead limbs, and anything else used to keep the fires going. Out of necessity, these baskets had to be strong and sturdy. It is not unusual to find old books with pictures of ladies and their baskets of peat.

Old pea basket painted white. 12" w, 18" l, 15" o.h. $55–$125

Old peat basket made of splints. $150–$250

Pen Basket

With the demise of the quill pen, the ink or fountain pen took its proper place in the scheme of writing. About the same time, the souvenir business was in full swing; so it was only natural that basketmakers would make pen baskets—baskets that not only fit the pens, but also fit neatly on one's desk. In the Northeast they were made of ash splint and sweet grass. They aren't that plentiful today, because, like so many of the 5-and-10-cent souvenirs of long ago, they weren't considered important enough to save.

Ash splint and sweet grass pen basket. 2" w, 7½" l, 1" h. **$9–$14**

Penobscot Indians

It would be difficult to say which of the four tribes—Micmacs, Penobscots, Maliseets, or Passamaquoddies—living in Maine makes the most or the best baskets. For centuries, they have all excelled in basketry. Many examples of their work can still be found, some of it absolutely exquisite. Penobscot

Old porcupine-quill box thought to have been made by the Penobscots. 3½" w, 5" l, 2½" h. **$125–$200**

women, who learned the art and craft of basketmaking from their mothers and grandmothers, are still making baskets. These women are also now teaching classes for those who want to learn basketmaking. For those who want to study the work and culture of the tribe, there is the Penobscot Indian Museum in Old Town, Maine.

The Penobscot Indian Nation is the oldest documented, continuously operating government in North America—a government that continues, today, with its unbroken succession of Chiefs and Governors.

The few very early examples of Penobscot work belong to descendants of the makers; therefore, it's difficult to find items to compare with the baskets made later. But it would be safe to assume that both designs and colors were changed to meet the com-

New Penobscot-made yarn basket, ash splint and sweet grass. 7" dia, 11½" h. **$50–$85**

157

Double-handled ash-splint basket. 4" dia, 5½" h. $25–$39

Ash-splint covered basket. 14" dia, 10" h. $57–$98

Penobscot-made work basket filled with ash splints; Unity College collection. $75–$125

Covered ash-splint basket. 15" dia, 10" h. $65–$135

petition around the turn of the century when the Penobscots began making baskets for the tourist trade. They didn't change the quality—it is still excellent.

The Penobscots lived in the same area as the Shakers, who would often farm out basketmaking jobs to Indians, and they would make the baskets to Shaker specifications. The Penobscots were very skilled and had to depend, to some extent, on the money coming in from their baskets. Thus, it is safe to assume that they made many items for the Shakers, and also, they may have made extras of that type to sell to their customers.

The Shakers went into towns and resort areas selling their baskets and other items, and they also had community stores at their farms. The Penobscots had roadside stands, and they sold at gift shops around the resorts.

Basketmaking hasn't changed much for the Penobscots in recent years, except that they have to travel further to find the fine ash trees required for their basketry. The men still go out and find the trees, cut them into lengths, and bring them home, where they pound them to separate the annual growth. From there, it is usually the work of the women to finish preparing the materials and then make the baskets, although some men still make baskets. Gathering sweet grass is a job for either the men or the women, and either can comb it after it is dry. The men are usually the ones who make the sweet-grass combs, the molds or forms, and the cutters.

The Penobscots not only excel in ash-splint and sweet-grass basketry, they also make birch-bark and porcupine-quill boxes. Their early work was so fine, an English visitor once wrote that they made "dishes of birch bark sewed with thread from spruse [spruce] and white cedar roots." The pieces were "decorated with *florisht* work." he wrote, "like glittering quills from the porcupine." He also mentioned that they were dyeing the quills in various colors, verifying an early use of both porcupine-quill decoration and the use of dyes, as this was written in the mid 1600s.

Peruvian Weave

Actually, the Peruvian weave is a variation of the lazy squaw weave, one that was described as easy in most basketry books.

Lazy squaw was the first weave described in the Indian basket-weaving book published in 1903. The only variation, they said, was the difference in the number of times the raffia was wound around the reed before the stitch was caught under the previous row. They suggested using raffia rather than the material used by the Navajo women. By varying the number of times the raffia was wound between the stitches, different designs and effects could be produced. The more raffia one used, the stronger the basket. Two variations of the Peruvian weave were the diamond pattern and the spiral pattern.

In some places, these raffia-covered reed baskets are sold as Indian-made. A few may be Indian-made, but the majority were made by women who followed instructions given in basketry books that offered to send a kit with an "already begun" basket. The ladies could order the kits with the baskets already started, and then complete them and have

Small, raffia-covered reed box in Peruvian weave. Note the button on the inside—it is used to hold the finial. 8½" dia, 2¼" h. $45–$95

what they considered to be Indian baskets. They would tell their families and friends that they had genuine Indian baskets, and that myth continues today.

Philippine Baskets, New

So many new baskets are coming from the Philippines now, it's difficult to keep up with them. Women in many areas are having "basket parties" on the order of the plastics and cosmetics parties. They go to each other's homes where they play games and see displays of the new baskets for sale. Most of the baskets seen have labels stating that they were made "exclusively for home parties" and, in smaller letters, that they were made in the Philippines. The baskets are well made, and they are inexpensive when compared to the finer, old baskets. Of course, this is one of the best arguments for studying all types of baskets before spending large sums of money. These baskets can be aged a bit on the outside, and it is going to be a tad difficult to separate them from some of the newer, expensive ones being made by the Indians of the Southwest, such as the one shown in the illustration here. The larger basket was made recently in the Philippines and sold at a basket party for $5. The smaller one was made recently by the Papago Indians and retails for $75. There is quite a difference between the two when you study them carefully, but at a glance, they seem quite similar.

This small basket is a new Papago-made; the large one was newly made in the Philippines.

Philippine-Made Baskets

It's nearly impossible to tell which of the old baskets were made in the Philippines and which were made in other Oriental countries. But there is no problem with the new Philippine-made baskets. They have labels listing the country of manufacture, and they are coming to the States in greater and greater numbers. See "Philippine Baskets, New."

Philippine-Made Purse

Before World War II, soldiers were stationed in the Philippines, and sailors came into the ports anytime their ships docked. Both were eager buyers of gifts for mothers, wives, and girlfriends back home. Purses were a favorite. They were both useful and showy—with the initials P.I. (Philippine Islands) on the side, everybody knew you had relatives in the service.

Basketry purse made of palm leaves. 5" w, 7" l, 7" h. $15–$18

The purse is made of some kind of palm leaves with a border, and the initials are in red and green. The purse appears to date from the late 1930s or early 1940s, and native dyes were probably being used on the islands. The purse is shaped like a doctor's bag and has two extra fasteners, one on either side of the handle.

Piassaba Fiber

Another name for *Piassava,* a coarse fiber made from several kinds of palm leaves. See "Piassava Fiber."

Piassava Fiber

A coarse fiber obtained from several different types of palm trees. In South America the fiber was used to make ropes, while in Europe it was used to make brooms for street sweeping.

It was also used to make some baskets. In 1925, a writer and basketmaker gave instructions for using the fiber in basketry. The writer claimed she was the first person to use piassava fiber in basketmaking. The fiber could be dyed to create designs, or it could be left relatively plain by simply using an arrow stitch when making the basket.

160

Basket made of piassava fiber. 8" dia, 5" h. $35–$44

Picnic Baskets or Hampers

Like sewing baskets, picnic baskets were made in a variety of shapes and sizes. Many picnic baskets made after the introduction of the automobile were designed especially to be used with cars. In fact, at least one is known to have the name of the car, Renault, stenciled in the inside cover.

They were made of every conceivable material. Some were plain, actually on the primitive side, while the later ones came complete with dishes, flatware, and woven bottle holders on the side. The fancy, fitted ones are still made today at one basket factory, and maybe at others as well.

Swing handle on a picnic basket.

Intriguing willow picnic basket with primitive lid fastener. 11" w, 17" l, 8" h. Damaged, $30–$50; good condition, $78–$105

Flat willow picnic basket. $59–$75

During the first part of the twentieth century, picnicking was considered the perfect date for young couples. Since there were so few forms of entertainment—no radio or TV, few picture shows, and so forth—a picnic was considered the perfect activity for a gentleman and his date.

Willow was one of the most popular picnic-basket materials, although many other materials were used. See "Willow, Picnic Basket."

Picture Frame

Old woven picture frames are scarce, but later wicker ones are plentiful. The frame in the picture dates from around 1920 and is believed to have been made by the Eskimos of Alaska. The grass used to make it, and the workmanship, closely resemble Eskimo work. When found, this picture frame contained a religious picture and a notation on the back that it was a confirmation gift, apparently for a French Canadian, as the message was in French and had a Canadian address.

Woven-splint pie basket (with mounted duck behind). 11" dia, 5" h. $25–$49

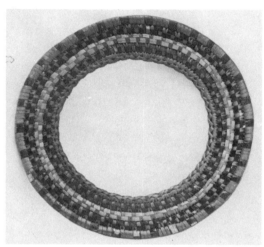

Picture frame woven of grass. 11" dia. $49–$85

Double-handled Passamaquoddy-made pie basket. 12" dia, 12" h. $35–$69

Pie Baskets

There weren't many bakeries years ago, so the housewife baked on her own. In fact, baking was one of the things she considered absolutely essential, and she never missed a chance to show off her baking skills.

She would pack her finest pies in a pie basket and off she would go to a church gathering, family reunion, or picnic in the meadow. The pies might be sweet or meat, and they might be packed in single- or double-decker pie baskets, with handles or without (they might even have double handles). They could be open or covered, but the majority were covered. The type of pie basket, like all other baskets, seemed to depend on the needs and desires of the user. Pie baskets were also used for cakes, and sometimes they were used as storage places for cakes and pies in the home. The pie basket was probably the forerunner of the later metal, aluminum, and plastic cake and pie containers.

Double pie baskets are usually the same size and shape as single baskets; they just have two sections so two pies can be taken in the same basket. They were quite popular with housewives with large families who had to take more than one pie to a church supper or social. It is believed the Micmac Indians

Double pie basket with double swing handles. 12" dia, 15" o.h. $88–$155

Reproduction willow gathering basket (front) and reproduction willow fish trap (back).

were the first to make pie baskets, but soon every basketmaker was making them. They are made of ash splints, not as thin and narrow as those used in the fancier baskets, but not as wide and thick as those used in gathering baskets.

Pilgrim Baskets, Reproductions

Years of research has gone into Plimoth Plantation, which is a re-creation of the village where the Pilgrims established homes after arriving on the Mayflower. The idea is to reproduce those early days so visitors today can step back in time and see how the Pilgrims lived. The houses are furnished authentically, the guides who represent the first Pilgrims go about everyday chores, and, to complete the picture, the guides only speak of things relating to that era, in Elizabethan English.

Women plant and harvest their gardens, especially the herb gardens, while the men work on new buildings or thatch the roofs on older ones. After much study and research, some baskets were made to represent those used by the Pilgrims. Using willow, the Pilgrims made both a two-handled basket for gathering corn and a fish trap for catching fish in the nearby streams and in the ocean.

Pincushions

From their arrival on the Mayflower to the turn of the nineteenth century, most American ladies made their own clothing or had it made by a dressmaker. This meant pins and needles were essential for everyone. Pins were not only essential, they were quite expensive for many years; thus, the housewife wanted to take care of the pins she had and wanted to know where to find them when she needed them. With that idea in mind, someone created the pincushion. Since they were handmade, they were made in many different styles and sizes and of many ma-

Round rattan cushion, $12–$25; sweet-grass cushion, $22–$40

Sweet-grass pincushion. 1½" dia, nearly 1" h. $7–$13

Velvet-topped Shaker pincushion. $50–$89

terials. When basketry was at its peak of popularity, pincushions were made of rattan with padded velvet tops, and in the Northeast they were made of ash splint with ribbon-bedecked satin tops. The Shakers made them using woven poplar.

Indians in the Northeast made pincushions similar to those made by the Shakers. After all, they were competing for the same

New Penobscot rocking-chair pin cushion, sweet grass and ash splint. 3½" w, 4" h. $18–$25

customers—the tourists. The Shakers used poplar strips woven together, while the Indians used sweet grass.

Pine Bark Strips

There are dozens of different kinds of pine trees growing all over the world. One species may furnish food (nuts); another lumber for house- and ship-building; and another tar, turpentine, and resin. Other pine trees furnish bark that's perfect for cutting into thin strips for weaving and plaiting into basketry items. The cones off some trees are used to make wreaths for Christmas decorations, and some of the small green pine trees are used for Christmas trees. Needles from the long-leaf pine are used by both white and Indian basketmakers.

Pine Cones

Long-leaf pine needles are used to make baskets and other basketry items, and the beautiful little pine cones are used to decorate them, giving them an overall pine look.

Old covered basket made of pine needles and decorated with small pine cones. 10" dia, 8" h. $50–$85

New Coushatta pine needle basket decorated with small pine cones and green raffia leaves. 9½" dia, 8¼" h. $35–$50

Some cones are left natural; others are painted bright colors before being attached to the pine needle or vine baskets.

Pine Needle Basketry

About 400 species of pine are known to grow all over the world, yet they have only been used extensively in the southern part of the United States to make basketry items. Only the long-needle variety, those measuring 12 to 20 inches long, can be used. They are most easily found under the trees known as long-leaf or slash pine.

Both the Indian and white basketmakers in the southeastern part of the country have long made baskets and novelty items using pine needles. They can be gathered during any time of year, but to get the best quality with the least trouble, they should be gathered in the late spring or early summer, as soon as they have reached full growth. Some basketmakers wait until fall—usually late fall or early winter—and then gather the pine needles that have fallen. If they are left too long, however, they will become brittle and be difficult to work with.

Each basketmaker had his or her own method of gathering. Some prefer to use the fallen needles after they have turned brown, while others prefer using them while they are still a bit green. An 82-year-old Coushatta man makes baskets while the needles are a bit green and uses no finish. The needles

New Miccosukee pine needle basket with doll head finial. 9" dia, 7" h. $100–$145

in his baskets looked as though they might become loose after drying out completely, but a year later they were as tight as the day the baskets were bought.

Early basketmakers stitched the coils of pine needles in their baskets with embroidery thread, a custom continued by the Miccosukee Indians in Florida. But most pine needle basketmakers today use raffia. It's also interesting that most white pine needle basketmakers finish their baskets with a solution of shellac, while Indians leave theirs natural.

Just as they have different ideas for gathering and finishing pine needle baskets, basketmakers have different methods for curing the needles. To get a rich brown color, the needles are left in the rain, sun, frost, and wind for as long as it takes for them to reach a rich, golden brown color. Or, if the basketmaker prefers green needles, as most Indian basketmakers do, they're left to dry away from the sun and rain, preferably in the house. Some makers remove the growth end of the needles, while others use them to an advantage in the design.

Pine Needle Pin or Brooch

Not only can nearly any material in the world be used to make baskets, but once it is thus used it can be used to make nearly anything. Proof of that is the pin or brooch.

This pin is in the shape of a basket and was probably made in the South, where pine needles are longer and more plentiful. It was bought in Maine. The pine needles were coiled and fastened together with light-green embroidery thread. To attach the pin to the back, the thread holding the first oblong coil was also fastened through the three eyes in the back of the pin.

Pine needle pin or brooch. 2" w, 2½" o.h. $8–$15

Pine Needle Stitches

Each basketmaker uses the stitches of his or her choice, but the basic pine needle stitches are plain, single split, wheat, leaf, wing, and fern.

Pitchers, Woven

No one has yet been able to explain why basketmakers wove pitchers, unless it was to prove that anything could be made in basketry. Or perhaps novelties like pitchers sold well. Many basketmakers supplemented their meager incomes by selling baskets, which means they made things they thought would sell. They also copied items made by other basketmakers, but one of the quickest ways to start an argument is to ask an old basketmaker who made a certain bas-

Oak-splint pitcher. 7" dia, 9" h. $200–$300

Ash-splint and sweet-grass pitcher, Unity College collection. 4" dia, 6" h. $90–$150

166

ketry item first. Each basketmaker claims to be the first, whether white or Indian.

Oak-splint pitchers were made in the Great Smoky and Ozark mountain areas. Ash-splint and sweet-grass examples were made in the Northeast.

Piticas

Double-woven and lidded baskets of beargrass, made by the Tarahumara Indians of northern Mexico. See "Tarahumara Indians."

Plaiting

Basketmakers of the Northeast use plaiting, or braiding, to weave sweet grass into the beautiful designs they use on their ash-splint baskets. Among the Indian basketmakers, the Micmacs, Mohawks, and Passamaquoddies seem to opt for the use of plaited or braided sweet grass fastened on the outside of their basketry items, while the Penobscots, Chippewas, and some other tribes prefer to include the designs in the baskets themselves.

Plaque or Tray

Probably made by the Hopis, this piece is equally at home as a plaque or tray. Or it

Wickerwork plaque or tray. 11½" dia. $65–$125

could have been the cover for a basket. Only one side has a design. The work is done in wickerwork and is quite colorful with lots of orange, green, black, and natural.

Plate, Basketry-Covered

Quite often, plates are seen encased in a basketry holder—the back of a plate is completely covered and a basketry rim extends around the front. First impression links this to imported products—and some probably are—but during the first and second decades of this century, when basketry was experiencing such a revival, instructions were given in several books for "covering a plate with vine, willow, or reed."

Plunder Basket

No special basket was made for this purpose; any old basket will suffice. Plunder basket is simply the name given an old basket used to hold *plunder,* which, as my grandmother described it, consisted of "things too good to throw away, yet not really good enough to keep." New baskets were seldom used as plunder baskets; instead, the beautiful old ones were relegated to this chore when they became too worn for their regular chores. My grandmother kept hers in the pantry of the old farm house.

Poarch Creek Indians

Like so many southern tribes, the Poarch Creek Indians were skilled in pine needle basketry, and they also used some cane in earlier days. They no longer make baskets. They are now involved in business—a bingo palace that enables them to buy and operate motels, restaurants, low-income housing, and a catfish processing plant—near the reservation at Atmore, Alabama. With only 1800 Poarch left on the reservation, most of them are working on the various businesses, leaving little time for basketmaking.

Pomo Indians

A century ago, California boasted 700,000 Indian inhabitants. Unlike other Indians, these people preferred the simple, peaceful life. Some were even described as lazy because they were content to utilize the available materials to fit their simple, everyday needs.

They all made baskets. Some like the Pomos made very exquisite baskets—very desirable baskets with decorations of beads, feathers, and shells. More than two years were required to make some of their beautiful baskets, and they also made other types of baskets, some rather plain. In fact, the Pomos were among the most versatile basketmakers, as they could combine both twining and coiling in so many different ways.

Originally, their name was Poma, *Po* for "red color" and *Ma* for "earth." They became known as "the people of the red earth," and then the name was changed to Pomo.

Old willow-wrapped basket is similar to those made by the Pomos. 9½" dia, 7" h. $50–$110

Popularity of Baskets

Only in the last 20 years has the number of basket collectors increased so rapidly. Prior to that time auctioneers seldom bothered with anything but the finest baskets in an estate sale, and even these were lumped together in the hopes they would bring a $5 or $10 bid for the lot. Collectors at that time were only interested in the finest baskets in pristine condition.

A search through stacks of antique publications from 1929 through 1965 has failed to uncover a single ad listing a basket for sale. It wasn't practical to pay for an ad to try to sell something that would only bring $5 or less and that had to be described rather thoroughly. Actually, not too many antique shops carried baskets as there wasn't that much demand.

But the picture has changed drastically in the past 15 to 20 years. Now it is said that quilts, dolls, and baskets are among the antiques with the fastest-growing popularity today. It is difficult to find a person who doesn't have a few baskets now. They may be contemporary and only used as decoration or in decoration, but they will be found in nearly every home in America.

Only excellent-quality baskets such as this were collected a few years ago. 12" w, 21" l, 13" o.h. $225–$365

Porcupine Weave or Design

Much confusion has arisen over the difference between porcupine weave or design and porcupine quill work. The former is a design created by curling ash splints into points, while the latter is when quills are removed from the porcupine and inserted into birch-bark boxes, belts, and other items.

Porcupine weave was introduced in the 1860s, but since the weave is difficult to do and is time-consuming, it has not been used as much in recent years. Old baskets with porcupine weave can be found quite often. Some are light in color, indicating they have been stored in attics and basements, shielded from air and light.

To make the porcupine weave, the basketmaker took both ends of a piece of paper-thin ash splint and turned them to the center. The next step was to roll the splint under, leaving a sharp point on the basket. The splint was passed under the weaver, given a sharp turn outward, another turn inward, and then passed under the next spoke. A plain weaver was worked along with it at the same time to keep the sides of the basket strong.

Porcupine-Quill Work

Porcupine-quill work is sometimes called simply *quill work*. It can be compared to embroidery, as the quills from a porcupine are worked in to form a design on birch bark.

The quills are removed from the dead porcupine and vary in length from $1\frac{1}{2}$ to 3 inches. The quills can also vary in diameter, but only by fractions of an inch. They are hollow, which means they can be used round, crushed flat, or split.

Ash-splint and sweet-grass basket with porcupine weave. $6\frac{1}{2}$" dia, $3\frac{1}{2}$" h. **$30–$64**

Finer quality ash-splint basket with smaller porcupine-weave design. 8" dia, $5\frac{1}{2}$" h. **$45–$90**

Birch-bark box with porcupine-quill butterflies. Sweet-grass trim around the edge (top). 4" dia, 2" h. **$95–$125.** *Canadian-made porcupine-quill box (bottom). 2" dia, 2" h.* **$65–$75**

Variegated green clover leaves decorate the top of this old birch-bark box. Leaves are made with porcupine quills. 2" w, 4" l, 1½" h. $75–$115

Porcupine-quill box, Unity College collection.

Old porcupine-quill box. 4½" dia, 2½" h. Damaged, $45–$75; good condition, $75–$150.

The first chore after the quills are plucked is to dry them and then sort and grade them according to quality and length. Then the quills are ready to be dyed. Surprisingly, porcupine quills can be dyed with the same vegetable dyes used in other basket materials. Today, porcupine-quill basketmakers use commercial dyes like all other basketmakers.

The Indians of the Northeast were the first to make quill boxes and baskets. Working with them is an art, and a rather difficult one to master, as the quills cannot be worked in a circle. The designs have to be made so the quills can be inserted either straight or in a geometric design. Flowers can be made, but the design has to be such that the quills are placed straight to form the round or pointed petals.

Since quillwork is very tedious and can be painful when the workers' fingers continue to be pierced by the sharp quills, it has been practiced on a limited basis. The quills are very sharp, and both ends have to be inserted into the birch bark. Workers can't wear gloves as they have to feel the quills working into place.

The birch bark is first cut to make whatever the maker wants, and then the quills are inserted into the design. Some makers are able to work with completed boxes, but most prefer doing the quill work first and then completing the box—lacing it together with spruce roots or basswood.

Once the box is cut, the design to be used is decided; then, the design is sketched on the bark. Quillwork cannot be done on a by-guess-and-by-gosh method if it is to be attractive. When the sketch is done, small holes are punched into the bark with the small awl. The holes have to be very close together, and there must be two—one for either end of the quill.

Quillwork was not used on birch bark only; in the early years, Indians used quill decorations on their leather clothing. The leather was stretched tight and the quills inserted into it. When it was removed from the frame, the leather naturally tightened, which kept the quills in place. The leather had to be lined with regular leather just as

*Birch-bark box with split-quill embroidery. 2½" w, 4" l, 2" h. Due to scarcity, **$150–$200***

*Old-ash-splint potato basket. 16" dia, 14" o.h. **$19–$30***

*New potato basket made by Micmacs. 17" dia, 15" o.h. **$26–$35***

the bark boxes have to be lined to hold the quills in place. A lining was necessary in the clothing to prevent the quills from scratching the wearer.

Most of the decorated quill boxes, like the regular birch-bark baskets and boxes, are fastened together with spruce root and sometimes basswood. Some have extra decorations of sweet grass.

It was not unusual for a basketmaker to split some of the porcupine quills used in the embroidery of a birch-bark box, but it was unusual to split all of them so that the work looked almost like moose-hair embroidery, as has been done in the example pictured. Split quills allowed the work to be done a little more in circles, making it look more delicate. The decorating method used was the same as for nonsplit quills, but with split quills the work was finer and more intricate.

Potato Baskets

Today, most potatoes are harvested by machine, but before machines, all potatoes were dug with hand tools by individuals. This chore required strong, sturdy baskets—the type of potato baskets the Micmacs and Maliseets have been making for years.

With only a small current demand for potato baskets on the farm, but with the increased popularity of baskets of all kinds, new potato baskets are appearing in gift shops

and restorations all around New England. They are now enjoying new prestige as wood or magazine baskets. Incidentally, they are quite similar to the rice baskets of Louisiana in both shape and size.

Potato Printing

This process is thought to have originated in Massachusetts, or possibly New Hampshire, and is called potato printing because potatoes were often used to make the designs (do the printing). A design was cut into the potato, which was dipped into dye and then pressed onto the basket splints. See "Block Printing."

171

Powaac Roots

Powaac is a root used by Indians to make yellow dye for basket materials. It makes a brilliant shade of yellow.

Pricing Baskets

Pricing a basket can be difficult, as there are several factors to consider. If a basket is collected with investment in mind, then only perfect examples should be considered. On the other hand, I sometimes buy a badly damaged basket for study purposes, especially if it is a rare example. Between those extremes are the average collectors who buy baskets because they like and enjoy them or they want to use them for a practical purpose.

There are also specialized collectors who collect only one type of basketry. They may collect only oak-splint baskets made in their area, or they might collect only one kind of basket, such as porcupine quill boxes. This narrows the field considerably and also affects prices. Scarce items in any field are more expensive than those that are plentiful.

Prices are also affected by locations. For instance, old baskets are much more plentiful in the northeastern part of the country than in other parts. There, ash-splint baskets are especially plentiful, and their prices are reasonable compared to prices in other areas. It is not unusual to find as many as two dozen fine-splint baskets in some shops in the area. Ash-splint baskets sell better in the Northeast because collectors are familiar with them. The same applies to cane and pine needle baskets of the Deep South. They are more plentiful there and more reasonably priced.

Quality, workmanship, and condition have a tremendous bearing on price. A basket made by a good basketmaker of quality materials that is still in good condition will always bring top dollar, regardless of the collector or location.

Not surprisingly, New England collectors want baskets made by basketmakers from their area as opposed to baskets from Canada. One of the best ways to distinguish between a basket made in New England and one made in Canada is to look closely at the dyed splints in the bottom. New England basketmakers dyed their splints after they were split, but Canadian makers split theirs after dyeing. The cutting after dyeing leaves a faint white edge on the splints, while the New England-made baskets have solid-color splints.

To further confuse the pricing issue, there is the story of two brothers with similar collecting interests. In the early 1980s, one brother died and his estate was sold at auction. One of his fine baskets sold for $3500. The other brother soon found that collecting alone was not as much fun. He was probably thinking about the prices his brother's collection brought, so he decided to sell his own collection at auction. When his baskets sold, one almost identical to his brother's $3500 basket sold for just $295. One auction-goer probably summed it up best with his statement, "Antiques from a dead collector always bring more than those from a live collector."

Prison-Made Baskets

Basketmaking is believed to be so therapeutic that it is now being taught in some prisons, and those prisons that don't have formal classes encourage prisoners to learn, if they are so inclined. Prisoners in the East lean toward the Nantucket Lightship method. The baskets they are making are excellent and can compete with older baskets, after the new ones have aged.

The basket in the photograph was made a couple of years ago by a young man in a Massachusetts prison who was trying to learn a trade so he could support himself when he was released. Apparently he has mastered the craft, because the workmanship is excellent, and with the demand today for these baskets he should be able to make a good living.

Prison-made oval basket after the Nantucket style. 5½" w, 8¼" l, 11" o.h. $45–$75

Ash-splint pumpkin baskets; large, 9½" dia, 7½" h, $95–$135; small, 4¼" dia, 3½" h, $25–$45

Puccoon Root

Another species of the bloodroot plant used to make an orangey-red dye for basket materials. The puccoon root was used more by basketmakers in the South than in the North.

Pumpkin-Shaped Baskets

Pumpkin baskets made by the Passamaquoddies (and maybe by other tribes) were not made for harvesting pumpkins, but were made as novelties. They were made to closely resemble pumpkins.

The large pumpkin basket is very realistic with its leaves and sweet-grass stem that doubles as a handle. The small one is adorable because of its size. To make them even more realistic, the ash splints used to make pumpkin baskets were dyed orange with dragon's blood, a powder that could be purchased in stores. Generally, dyes were made from materials gathered in the forest and fields, but in the case of the basket shown here, the Passamaquoddies probably bought the dye in order to get a true orange to rep-

resent the true color of a pumpkin. These pumpkin baskets were made during the heyday of the tourist trade, and the basketmakers probably thought the truer orange color would make them sell better.

Purses or Handbags

Prior to the 1850s, women had little use for purses or handbags. They raised most of their food and made their own clothing, and if the wife made a large purchase, her husband paid for it. She sold or bartered her eggs, milk, and butter for the few small things she wanted at the store. Most women used little or no makeup and carried no keys or other items found in purses today. They wore aprons with pockets in which they carried snuff boxes or tobacco for their pipes.

When ready-made purses became available, they were usually ugly little black or brown leather things, called *satchels*. Satchels would be totally unsatisfactory today, and they probably weren't that popular with the ladies of those days, judging by the number of purses they made for themselves—purses of velvet, satin, and other fabrics to match their clothing.

By the turn of the century, the purse was an accepted part of milady's outfit, and everybody began making a version of the perfect purse.

During the ensuing years, all kinds of purses were made, but the ones of most interest to basket collectors today are those made of basketry materials—ash splints,

Chitimacha cane purse, zipper top. $350–$500

Purse made by the same method and using the same materials as the teapot caddy, willow sewing basket, wine cradles, and hamper. Has leather trim and label in the top showing it was hand-made for exclusive wholesaler in New York. Smaller bags of the same type have been seen with labels indicating they were made in Hong Kong. $7\frac{1}{2}$" w, 10" l, 6" h. $10–$19

Circa 1930 purse woven after the egg-basket style. Painted white with design added on the hinged top. $6\frac{1}{2}$" w, $9\frac{3}{4}$" l, 9" o.h. $25–$35

Chitamacha envelope-type purse. $350–$500

sweet grass, and cane, or a combination of these materials.

Basketmakers of the Northeast were probably the first to get into the commercial aspect of basketry purses. They had customers ready to buy—the tourist trade. Southern Indians also made purses, and some of the most beautiful ones were made by the Chitimachas of Louisiana. They made at least two styles, but both were more or less the clutch-style purse. One style had a zipper across the top, while the other was an envelope type.

Purses continued to be made by hand and were hand-decorated. Copies of the Nantucket baskets were made during the

forties and fifties in purse form. Also, about that time, a factory-made basketry purse was available to be decorated by people with a flair for painting. Anything could be painted— scenes of the local town, a restoration, or whatever one chose.

Factory-made basketry purse with scenes of Westville, Georgia, restoration painted around the bottom. 5½" w, 9½" l, 9" h. $15–$25

Well-decorated ash-splint purse, Unity College collection. $39–$59

Ash-splint, sweet-grass, and Hong Kong grass purse. 5½" w, 10" l, 7½" h. $19–$35

Pussy Willow

A species of willow used from time to time to make baskets is the *pussy willow*. It's not as satisfactory as regular willow, but some pussy willow baskets are still being made today. As the willow dries, the weavers shrink, leaving wide spaces in the basket. These can be filled with more weavers, but the baskets are never as satisfactory as those made with regular willow.

Quillwork

Another name for basketry items using porcupine quills. See "Porcupine Quill Work."

Rabbit Brush

Indians used the branches of rabbit brush to make finely woven baskets. This plant was given the name *rabbit brush* because its dense growth provides a refuge for the jackrabbits that inhabit areas of the western United States in which the plant grows.

Raffia

Raffia is the name given to a material obtained from a group of palms that flourish in Madagascar and the surrounding islands. Also spelled *raphia*.

The trees often grow to heights of 75 feet; about 50 feet of it is perfect for making raffia, which is the outer cuticle of the palm. Raffia is a tough, beige-colored material that is cut into strips like thin fabric. It is soft and flexible, easily dyed, and is easy to use. Modern basketmakers—especially in Alabama, Louisiana, and Mississippi—still use this material. Its durability and adaptability are an asset. Raffia is used to embroider shoes, hats, and purses, as well as baskets. Many of the basket books published around the turn of the century suggested that one could use round reeds wrapped in raffia to make an imitation Indian basket.

Fifty years ago, raffia could be bought in at least 25 different colors. Many basketmakers, though, preferred dyeing their own raffia in order to obtain colors that were softer and better suited to what they were making. Dyes that wouldn't work well on other basket materials worked perfectly on raffia. For instance, tea and coffee produced a nice brown, iris petals produced purple, and heather produced a nice yellow. Leaves of the poplar tree produced a different shade of yellow; lily-of-the-valley leaves, and elder

This box was lined by hand to make a sewing box.

A Shaker artist could have painted the design on the top and sides of this box, and lined it. $4\frac{3}{4}$" w, $7\frac{3}{4}$" l, 2"h. $28–$48

Heart-shaped box with straw doll. $4\frac{1}{2}$" w, 5" l, 2" h. $25–35

and walnut shells, produced varying shades of green. Dandelion roots were used to make red dye for raffia.

Raffia-Wrapped Grass Boxes

These boxes of unknown origin are often confused with the woven-poplar Shaker boxes. In fact, it is not unusual to find them labeled "Shaker." They're not Shaker. Some have Oriental designs painted on them, and one person reported seeing one with a label from a German candy company. These gift boxes appear to date from the first few decades of the twentieth century.

Although they definitely are not Shaker, one of the brethren of the local Shaker Community (an expert on Shaker history) thought some of the boxes might have been decorated with designs that were handpainted by one of the sisters at the Canterbury, New Hampshire, community. He said she was a prolific painter and would paint designs on just about anything. It's very possible she painted floral designs on some of the raffia-wrapped grass boxes to make them more attractive. Also, it is possible that some of the boxes she painted were sold in Shaker stores. The boxes, however, were not made by the Shakers.

One immediately noticeable difference between these gift boxes and those made by Shakers is the type of hinge on the boxes. These boxes have wire hinges, whereas the Shaker woven-poplar boxes all had lids fastened on with ribbons—they were always tied. In the early days, sisters of the Shaker

Another style box with design painted on top. 4" w, 9" l, 2" h. $19–$35

community complained about the amount of time required to punch holes with a hand punch. Later, one of the brethern designed and made a punch that could be attached to a table, which was much faster and much easier to use. According to one report, that invention was shared with other Shaker communities where poplar baskets were made.

Raised Ring Inside Bottom

It's not too unusual to find small baskets with this type woven ring on the outside of the bottom, but it is unusual to find it on the inside.

Raised ring inside a feather basket.

Rattan

Rattan comes from one of a number of species of climbing palms that have long, round, solid-jointed stems. Rattan can be purchased in round or flat strips and comes in sizes numbered from 1 to 15. This convenience allowed the old basketmakers a wide range of sizes from which to select. It's tough, pliable, and long lasting.

The flat strips were used most often to make seats in chairs. Both the flat and round strips were used in basketry, with the majority being used by the later basketmakers who joined the turn-of-the-century revival. Many of the makers were urban housewives who found it easier to buy basket materials than to try and go out and gather them. Rural people felt it was a waste of money to

Red Basket, Oak

This is a sturdy, factory-made red oak work basket made to be used for carrying small but heavy loads. It appears to be 40 to 50 years old and, at one time, had paper of some kind glued around the top. Remnants of the paper can still be seen.

Rattan sewing basket. $20–37

This entire basket is still bright red—dyed, not painted. 6½" square, 4" h. $39–$55

Rattan basket with wooden beads. 13" h, 12½" dia. $10–$20

Factory-made red oak-splint basket. 11" w, 17" l, 11" o.h. $17–$38

buy rattan or any other basketry materials. They continued to go into the woods and fields, as they always had, to get free basket materials.

Redbud

A shrublike tree whose branches make excellent basketry material. Bears small, budlike pink flowers and is also known as *Judas tree*. See "Judas Tree."

Reed Sweet Grass

Unlike the sweet vernal grass that grows in pastures and meadows, reed sweet grass grows alongside lakes and streams. In England, it's cut two or three times a year, not only to make grazing land for cattle, but to bale as hay. In the early days of America, reed sweet grass was probably treated the

Basket with porcupine decoration and sweet-grass handle and rim, Unity College collection. $35–$67

Basket repaired with leather straps, long ago. $20–$25

Ash-splint basket filled with sweet grass ready for basketmaking. $59–$90

same way, but later it began to be used almost exclusively as basketmaking material. It is believed to be the sweet grass preferred by most basketmakers, and it has a sweet fragrance that lingers for years—even when used in basketry.

Reinforced Splint Basket

Baskets were reinforced in various ways when they were to be used for heavy chores, but the one pictured is a bit unusual in that the splints come all the way up the sides without being worked into the basket proper. It is made of oak splints and has been used for tough chores. Apparently it was left in a barn or damp basement as there is some damage in the bottom. The rim is nailed on, and the swing handle is fastened with metal rivets.

Oak-splint, swing-handle basket. 14" dia, 19" o.h. Damaged, $75–$100; good condition, 100 percent more.

Repairing Baskets

Prior to around 1975, baskets were so cheap and the supply so plentiful that nobody looked at damaged baskets unless they wanted one to paint or use for a flower pot. The picture has changed completely. The supply of fine old baskets is dwindling, and prices have soared. Now there is more and more talk of repairing baskets.

At auctions and antique shows, sellers will often point out repaired places on the finer baskets. Some of the repair work is so good, it seems rather pointless to mention it. On the other hand, other repair work was obviously done by someone unskilled.

Years ago, the finer baskets were repaired, although, generally, it was better to make or buy new ones. Even then, some repairs were crude.

Sweet grass is probably too difficult to repair, but broken splints can usually be replaced or repaired. Antique dealers specializing in old baskets seldom pass up badly damaged baskets that sell for a few dollars. These baskets can be taken apart and the splints soaked to make them pliable again so they can be reworked into slightly damaged baskets of the same material. With the fine old baskets disappearing into private collections, and prices sky-rocketing, it's a safe bet that the repairing of old baskets will become as popular as wicker repairing.

Reticule, Porcupine Quill Work

Reticule is the old name for ladies' purses or handbags. It was the name given to most of the early purses, especially the little brown and black leather ones used around the middle of the 1800s, and later. This one dates from around 1875, or maybe a little earlier, and was probably made by the Penobscot Indians.

The design and workmanship are good, but time has wreaked havoc with the quills on the back and on the bottom. It is made of three pieces of birch bark—two sides and a long piece that forms the bottom and is on either side. Colors are white, black, and rust. The seams where the pieces were joined is covered with what appears to be ribbon, a gesture towards covering the "seamy" side. Remnants of ribbon that were originally part of the handle remain. On the back where the quills are gone, the design drawn in pencil by the maker is still quite visible.

Porcupine quill reticule. Damaged, $50–$75; good condition, 100 percent more.

Rib-Type Splint Basket

This is just one of a dozen varieties of the rib-type baskets made in Appalachia and Pennsylvania, and possibly in other areas as well. It has a buttocks or gizzard shape, after a fashion, yet most of these baskets are larger than the usual buttocks basket.

The basket pictured is very similar to the baby carrier basket except that this type is smaller and has cupped ends. It could have been used for a small baby, while the larger one was probably for an older baby. It also could have been used as a gathering basket. The basketmaker made the handle twisted, rather than using one strong splint.

Rib-type splint basket. 14" w, 19" l, 15" h. $75–$119

Rice Baskets

We tend to think of rice as an Oriental dish, but Indians were eating it long before the white man arrived. This is especially true of the Indians living in the Great Lakes region of the country, where conditions were not favorable for raising corn. Since they couldn't raise maize, as did other tribes, they depended on the semiaquatic plants growing wild along the edges of the lakes and in the backwaters of the rivers. It is not known what the Indians called wild rice at that time, but the early settlers called it wild oats and wild wheat.

They didn't have to plant or tend wild

Old splint and cane rice basket. 16" dia, 10" h. $55–$115

rice; nevertheless, harvesting and preparing it could be an arduous task, beginning with guarding the wild crops from the birds. To keep birds from eating it, the women and girls would tie several stalks of the rice together with basswood twine. When it had matured, the rice was cut and carried home in birch bark canoes. Upon arriving home, the rice had to be hulled, dried, and smoked.

It's not known if the early Indians made a special basket just for rice, but they probably did. When the Cajuns (French Canadians) moved to Louisiana, they began growing rice, and they made baskets for gathering it. Today, rice is grown commercially and harvested by machines. Rice baskets—like so many other harvesting and storage baskets—are no longer needed, but the desire to collect them lingers on.

In Louisiana, the owner described the basket in this photograph as an old rice basket without a handle, that was carried under the arm while the worker gathered rice. Holding the basket under the arm while using it has given this rice basket a decidedly warped appearance. Strangely enough, this basket is made of two materials seldom seen in one basket—hickory splints and swamp cane. The spokes are made of splints; the weavers are made of cane.

Rice baskets are similar to Maine potato baskets, but the latter have handles. The spokes and weavers are also wider and thicker, as they must carry more weight.

Rice-Straw Basket

These baskets are a product of the China trade and date from around the nineteenth century. They came in two styles: plain and decorated. The latter had rather stylized flowers in bright colors and often were wrongly attributed to the Pennsylvania Dutch. The Pennsylvania Dutch may have decorated some of these baskets, but they are believed to have all been made in the Orient. The plain ones have been attributed to the Shakers, who sold them in their stores but did not make them. They look rather fragile, but the look is deceiving as they are well made and exceptionally strong.

Plain rice-straw basket. 7" w, 11" l, 6½" h $33–$57

Riddle

A *riddle* is a coarsely woven sieve primarily thought of as being used to separate chaff from grain. Some riddles were used in foundries and mines for sifting coal. There can be no doubt that the one pictured here was used in either a foundry or a mine, as it is covered with thick, black dust that could only come from years of exposure to coal.

Old splint riddle, 18" sq, 5" h. Used for coal.

Well-made splint riddle. 12" dia, 6" h. $70–$135

Rope Basket

Tough Manila rope, made of Manila hemp, was used by farmers, cattlemen, and others. The hemp was made from the leafstalk of a tree grown in the Philippines, one related to the banana palm. At one time, hemp was used to make paper. Still later, someone invented a rope-twisting or braiding machine. The rope was not tightly twisted, but it was a boon for farmers who could now make cheap, but usable, rope. It appears that someone braided the hemp and then sewed it together to make the basket shown in the photograph.

Braided twine or rope basket, late. 5" dia, 6½" h.
$10–$15

Runners

Although the farmer and his wife might make their own baskets, they were a frugal lot who didn't want to waste anything and had better things to do with their time than to

Round basket with crossbar of runners.

Square basket with three runners.

constantly make new baskets to replace those that had worn out. Therefore, they devised ways to ensure basket longevity. For carrying heavy loads, they used stronger handles and thicker splints. (Of course, over a certain thickness they would be too thick and heavy to weave, so there was a cutoff point.) To reinforce baskets and allow them to be pushed or pulled along the ground or floor, the frugal farmers added heavy splints on the bottom. These extra pieces were called runners, cleats, drags, or heels, depending on the location of the people using them.

Rush

Rush includes any plant of the genus *Juncus*. Rush plants include many which are found in low, marshy areas. Cattail and flag are often lumped under this title. In the Northern Hemisphere, some rush plants are tall and slender without leaves, while others have broad leaves. The stalks are used for making mats and baskets, and for caning chairs. A softer species of rush was grown in Japan and used exclusively for making mats.

Rush, like cattail, can be split and dyed to make baskets. Rush should be gathered when it reaches full growth and while the

183

stalk is still green. Old basketmakers knew the rush was ready for cutting when the tips of the leaves began turning brown. In most areas, this occurs around the middle of August. To prepare it for basketmaking, the rush was cut and tied in loose bundles, and then thoroughly dried, either in the shade or in a dark room.

Rye Baskets

Coiled rye baskets are more easily found north of the border states of Tennessee and Kentucky. They can still be found in rather plentiful supply in Pennsylvania, where they are believed to have originated. If old coiled rye baskets are not available, there are plenty of new ones. Old ones were made and used in New England and are fairly plentiful in that area today, along with some new ones. Some rye baskets are small and delicately made, while others are found with coils an inch thick. Rye baskets are still not as popular, nor as expensive, as splint baskets. Generally, they will be found priced from $25 to $125, depending on size, workmanship, and condition. As with all antiques, you can sometimes find a bargain. My bargain is shown in the picture below.

Rye basket, 10″ dia, 8″ h. $28–$60

Sabbathday Lake Shaker Trademark

Not all Shaker-made poplar items have trademarks, but it is believed that most of those made at the Sabbathday Lake community in Maine are so marked. The woven poplar boxes were made at the Alfred, Maine, community, but none has been seen with a trademark. Since freezing temperatures were necessary to condition the splints, it is possible that the boxes were made only at the Maine, New Hampshire, and New York communities.

Trademark found on the bottom of Sabbathday Lake woven-poplar boxes.

Saddle Basket

This name for the buttocks or gizzard basket came into use because this type of basket rode so well when tied on the saddle horn. See "Buttocks Basket."

Saddle Basket Design

The Cherokees still use the old materials and designs (named designs) in their basketry. The basket pictured is a fruit basket made of oak splints and dyed with walnut and bloodroot. The design is called "Saddle Basket."

184

Oak-splint fruit basket in Saddle Basket design. 6½" dia, 8" h. New ones, $24–$40; older ones, $50–$75.

Ash-splint and sweet-grass sandwich basket, Unity College collection. $43–$75

Sandstone

Sandstone is a coarse-grained rock used mostly in buildings. It is also used for whetstones and grindstones, but its most important use for basketmakers is as a fine-grained stone for smoothing basket materials. The Hopi used it extensively, as did some other tribes.

Sandwich Basket

The same basket that was used for cakes could be used for sandwiches. Like the uncovered cake basket, the sandwich basket was kept in the home and used to serve sandwiches on the veranda or in the gazebo.

Sassafras

The small tree that supplied sassafras tea for our ancestors also furnished bark to use in basketmaking. *Sassafras*, any of a number of related trees of the *laurel* family, is easily identified by its yellow flowers and bluish fruit. The dried roots of the sassafras are used for both medicine and flavoring. Its reddish-brown bark is tough enough for spokes and can be split to make weavers.

Scale Basket

These baskets were made by the Indians of northern Maine and were used mostly in fish-processing plants to hold fish scales, which would later be used in the manufacture of cosmetics.

Workmanship on these baskets is good but not outstanding, perhaps because of the type of work for which they were used. The type of wood used is not known, but they have durable white ash handles. It is possible that the basket is also made of ash but due to the fact that it has been wet for so long, it doesn't look like ash. Scale baskets are large, cumbersome, and not very attractive, so modern usage is limited. They make good log baskets because they are heavy.

A half dozen of these baskets were seen on a one-day trip to various antique malls in southern Maine. The prices asked for them explains in part why it is so difficult to pre-

Scale basket. 17½" dia, 15" h. $8–$60

pare an accurate price guide. The first two were priced at $35 each, the third at $8, the fourth at $25, the fifth at $60, and the last one at $40.

Scissor Sheaths

This is another of the souvenirs that basketmakers made during the tourist-trade days. Small, sharp-pointed scissors were

Scissor sheaths. Large with embroidery scissors, 2½" l. New, $5–$8; old, $10–$15. Smaller sheaths, 2" l. New, $4–$7; old, $10–$12.

necessary for fancy handwork, and ladies visiting friends often took their handwork with them. Unless the points of the scissors were covered, they could damage the work inside the sewing basket or damage the basket itself. The solution was an ash-splint and sweet-grass sheath for the scissors. Scissor sheaths are again being made by the Senecas, and maybe by other basketmakers as well.

Scottish Baskets

The Swedes gave this name to the broody hen basket. See "Hen Basket."

Scrap Basket

Old name for a wastepaper basket. See "Wastebaskets."

Seal Gut

Seal gut was traditionally used by the Alaskan basketmakers to add fancy designs on baskets. See "Eskimo Baskets."

Sedge

Sedge grows throughout the United States and one species seems to thrive in the sandy lands of the southern part of the country. Both the Indians and whites have long praised it as a multipurpose basketry material. It can be used to make yellow dye; the long, tough, woody interior of the roots is used to make white designs on coiled baskets. The flexible grass stems can be used for coiling.

Seminole Indians

The Muskhogean family of Indians, of which the Seminoles are members, was one of the great Indian families of the South. Before the arrival of the later southern aristocracy,

Coiling a grass basket.

Completed pine needle basket. 10" dia, 8" h.
$90–$125

these were the Indian aristocrats of the South. Alabama, Georgia, Mississippi, and parts of Tennessee were considered their territory until the white settlers came.

At first, the Muskhogean moved to Florida, because it was owned by the Spanish and they thought it would be safe. Florida was then sold to the United States, and after many battles and skirmishes, some of the Seminoles agreed to go to Oklahoma. Those who didn't agree (there were quite a few), instead fled to the Everglades, where they are today.

The Seminoles, like the Miccosukees, make baskets of coiled pine needles sewn together with waxed thread. They also make a frame of bark or cypress over which they

arrange their hair to achieve a hat-brim effect.

Seneca Grass

Another common name given to the sweet grass (*Hierochloe odorata*) used in many ways, but mostly in basketry. It is possible that the Seneca Indians first used the grass in their basketry, hence the name. See "Sweet Grass."

Seneca Indians

Six tribes—the Mohawks, Onondagas, Oneidas, Cayugas, Senecas, and Tuscaroras—made up the Six Nations, and all were excellent basketmakers. Many are still making baskets much as they did a century or so ago. There was and still is some variation in the baskets made by the various tribes. There are even minor differences between baskets made on neighboring reservations, but overall the baskets are basically alike.

As in most of the other tribes, both Seneca men and Seneca women made baskets, but usually the men cut the trees and prepared the splints, while the women did most of the weaving. The Senecas used fewer tools than did any of the other basketmakers. They used an axe to cut and remove the annual layers of the ash. Unlike so many other basketmakers, they preferred a straight-blade jackknife to a crooked knife, and they didn't

Storage basket similar to those made by the Senecas. 30" sq, 17" h. $59–$89

Ash-splint storage box or basket with removable cover. 12" w, 36" l, 18" h. $64–$89

Large oak-splint serving tray. 15" w, 20" l. $120–$175

Oak-splint tray with a reinforced strip through the center. 14" w, 23" l. $135–$200

want the knife to be too sharp, because if it slipped it could cut the worker or damage the splints. Some of the women used basket gauges for cutting the smaller splints, but others believed that the gauges not only wasted material, but also left the edges rough. The latter group preferred scissors. The only other tool used by the Seneca basketmakers was a screwdriver or other blunt instrument used to separate the warp and allow the binding through to the other side.

Interestingly, the Senecas made at least three types of sieves. One was very fine and was a flour sifter. The other two were hominy sifters, one made of twilled plaiting and the other using a hexagonal weave. There may have been other types, as well.

Serving Tray

Among the many things that can be made of woven oak splints is the serving tray, and basketmakers take great pride in their handiwork when making these trays. While other types are less expensive, handmade serving trays are often preferred. Serving trays were especially popular as late as the 1950s, when there was quite a bit of entertaining in the home. The basketry tray was handy for serving anything from hors d'oeuvres at a party to lemonade on the porch. Serving trays have been made of most basketry materials, including rattan and splints. Some later versions were made of pine needles with seashell scenes beneath their glass-

covered bottoms. These were made primarily for the tourist trade.

Set of Rib-Type Baskets, Painted

Probably on the theory that "old red" paint would make this set of baskets sell better and for more money, somebody painted them a weird shade of red, not exactly old red. At best this color would only fool the novice. These baskets are rather attractive and a change from natural-colored baskets. In fact, worked in with the color scheme of a room they could be extremely attractive.

Set of rib-type baskets. Largest 13" w, 21" l, 13" h; medium 11" w, 18" l, 11" h; small 10" w, 14" l, 10" h. $95–$135 set

Sewing Baskets

If one were to take a survey on the subject, the results would probably show that sewing baskets were made in a wider variety of shapes, styles, and materials than any other type of basketry item.

Ash-splint and sweet-grass sewing basket attributed to the Passamaquoddies. 9¼" dia, 5" h. $45–$80

The inside of a sewing basket, showing the pockets.

Sewing basket of ash splints turned to look like flower petals; Unity College collection. $49–$84

There were open sewing baskets and closed sewing baskets, as well as those in round, square, and oblong shapes. Some had handles; others didn't. Some were made plain, while others were fitted with places for needles, thread, pincushions, and scissors.

Sewing baskets were popular because everyone needed at least one, sometimes two. Even young girls needed sewing baskets. Ever since the Mayflower landed at Plymouth Rock, American girls have been taught to sew. Sometimes they learned fancy stitchery, other times plain sewing, but they had to learn it all because they needed to know how to make clothes for themselves and for their families when they set up homes of their own. They learned fancy stitchery so they could fill their hope chests and, later, make beautiful things for their own homes. Many parents believed that "Idle hands are the devil's workshop," so to keep those hands busy, they sewed and had their children sew. Sewing baskets were not necessarily designed to be beautiful and long lasting, just convenient. If a child came from a basketmaking family, chances are she made her own sewing basket. If not, an older sibling or parent might make a basket for her.

The child's sewing basket shown in the photograph is made of rattan, ash splint, and Hong Kong grass. It dates from around 1930. The drawstring top is designed to prevent

189

Child's sewing basket. 6½" dia, 7" o.h. $15–$27

the child from spilling the contents of her bag, should she drop it.

Prior to the invention of the sewing machine in the mid-1800s, all clothing and household linens were made by hand. Sewing baskets were essential and were used frequently, almost daily. The ladies were as involved in mending old things as they were in making new ones.

The very first "sewing baskets" were simply conventional baskets used to hold sewing items. They were made of whatever materials were available in the area—oak splints, hickory splints, pine needles, cane, and vines in the South; ash splints, sweet grass, willow, birch bark, and reed in the North. In the Southwest, basketmakers used willow, yucca, and whatever other grasses were available.

After the basketry revival around the turn of the twentieth century (when instruction books on basketry began to be published), reed and raffia were suggested as the best and easiest materials to find and use for making baskets. It was also at about this time that bamboo sewing baskets began to be imported in large numbers.

Today, old sewing baskets are quite collectible. Some are still used as they were originally intended, while others are used for other purposes. Some are perfect for dried-flower arrangements, and some of the old willow sewing baskets make great fruit

Three-finger, wooden Shaker sewing basket lined with satin and fitted with satin pincushion and woven poplar needle case; has Sabbathday Lake trademark. 12" l, 7½" w, 10" o.h. $250–$450

Covered ash-splint sewing stand. 13" dia, 24" h. $125–$150

190

baskets. One young girl uses several different kinds of covered sewing baskets to hold her costume jewelry.

Sewing Stands

Sewing and mending were most important in the early days of this country, so both sewing baskets and sewing stands were made. Stands, like the baskets, were made of many materials and in many styles. In many cases, they are woven of the same materials. Some are now classified as wicker, but since there is actually only a slight difference between the two, they can be classified and used together. Some were made during the Roaring Twenties. What is now

Wicker sewing stand with wicker chair. Stand, $190–$250.

Ash-splint sewing stand with square containers. 12" sq, 29" h. $140–$180

Ash-splint sewing stand with round containers; Unity College collection. $150–$175

called *wicker* furniture was, at that time, called *basket furniture*.

Beautiful sewing stands were made by basketmakers in the Northeast. The legs were usually made of hardwood, while the two containers were made of ash splints. Most of these have the decorative looping found on other ash-splint baskets. Some of the stands are open; others are covered.

Shaker Baskets

Today, with the growing interest in anything Shaker, it's not unusual to see ordinary baskets labeled or described as "Shaker" or "Shaker-type." In an attempt to educate the public, much has been written about Shaker baskets. Several collectors have pointed out how easy it is to mistake the bushwhacker or Taconic baskets with those made by the Shakers, and vice versa.

The Shakers made and sold thousands of baskets in their community stores scattered throughout New England, Kentucky, and Ohio. They also sold thousands of baskets they bought from individual basket-

Cat's head basket made after the Shaker style. 9½" dia, 12" o.h. $95–$125

makers who made them to Shaker specifications. The average basketmaker made the complete basket from start to finish, but the Shakers worked on a production line of sorts (maybe it should be called a community effort). A completed basket was not an individual accomplishment; instead, each person did the job for which he or she was best qualified or trained.

The Shakers were organized by Mother Ann Lee. They arrived in North America, from England, in 1774. Shortly thereafter, they began making ash-splint baskets, a craft they are believed to have learned from the Indians.

The Shakers were an industrious and ingenious people, so they were soon designing and making their own styles of baskets. It is not known when the Shakers first became interested in commercial ventures, but by 1816 they had established a reputation for excellent workmanship and quality, and the demand for their handmade items had increased to the point where they had stores in most of their communities. The Shakers sold their handmade items in the stores and later established routes through which they sold them.

Sometime after 1850, demand shifted from the larger utilitarian baskets to smaller, fancier baskets—the type that appealed to "summer people" (people who spent their summers in the nearby resorts). As the demand grew, the Shaker community streamlined its operation. In order to speed up the supply, each person was assigned the job he or she was most qualified to do.

Basketmaking continued at the Shaker communities for several decades; then, as the number of residents in the communities began to decline (they were a celibate order), and the demand for baskets lessened, they made fewer and fewer baskets.

One style among the various styles of baskets made by the Shakers was the *cat's head*—so named because the bottom of it resembled a cat's head. A smaller version was called a *kitten's head*. Other styles were the *spoon basket,* a miniature basket with cupped sides that resembled a spoon; a hexagon-weave cheese basket; a set of nesting baskets that vaguely resembled the Nantucket Lightship baskets; a so-called *deaconess* basket that was actually a well-made oblong basket, similar to some market baskets; fruit and apple baskets; and perhaps the most interesting of all, the baskets made to hold wood chips for the stoves. A wood-chip basket was placed in each room of the house. The most intriguing feature of the wood-chip basket was the pair of wooden strips attached along each side of the bottom of the basket so that it could "skate" along on snowy pathways rather than having to be carried by the handle. Also taken into account when the basket was designed was how heavy it would be when filled with wood chips, so handles were attached to both ends of the oblong basket.

Most baskets made by the Shakers had stationary handles; few, if any, had swing handles.

Shaker Boxes

Alfred

Two Shaker communities were located within 50 miles of each other in southern Maine. One was Sabbathday Lake, near New Gloucester, now operating in a limited capacity; the other was near Alfred, Maine.

Both communities made poplar strip boxes, but with a slight difference. Those made at Sabbathday Lake had the woven poplar strips glued on cardboard, while the

Inside of smaller box, pink satin lining, 6¼" sq, 2¼" h. $125–$225

Small Shaker woven-poplar box. 3½" sq, 2" h. $150–$250

Large Shaker woven-poplar box. 10" sq, 3¼" h. $175–$300

ones made at Alfred had the woven poplar strips glued on a wooden foundation. Such boxes may have also been made at other Shaker communities, but those with wooden foundations, although unmarked, are usually attributed to Alfred. Like those made

Woven poplar splint box made at Alfred, Maine, Shaker community around the turn of the present century. 3" w, 5" l, 2" h. $95–$145

Woven Shaker poplar box. 3½" sq, 2" h. $125–$195

at Sabbathday Lake, they also have white leather trim, and the tops are tied on with ribbon.

Sabbathday Lake

Since the dictionary defines a basket as a container made of interwoven twigs and rushes, thin strips of wood, and other flexible materials, the beautifully woven-poplar boxes made by the Shakers would have to be included in basketry books.

It's easy to appreciate the intricacy of Shaker boxes simply by looking at them, but when collectors learn of the long, tedious work required to make them, their appreciation grows.

Chores around the Shaker community were given to those best qualified for the job; therefore, the first step in making boxes was to assign the best woodsmen the chore of selecting the finest poplar trees (they would only use trees growing in moist land). Once the trees were cut, they were taken to the sawmill to be cut into lengths of 24 inches—no more, no less. The next step was to remove the bark and cut the lengths of wood into blocks that measured about 2½ square inches.

The Shaker men soon discovered that poplar blocks could be cut into much smoother, paper-thin pieces if they were kept frozen, so the wood was stacked outside and even covered with water to assure freezing.

The first chore relegated to the women

was culling imperfect strips and then sorting them. Not surprisingly, baskets were used in the basketmaking process—splints were taken by the basketful to the laundry room to be dried.

At first, the number of Shaker boxes to be made was limited to the amount of wood obtained from 17 logs. But when sales increased and production reached its peak, the Shakers were using three to four cords of wood per year.

Cutting, drying, and sorting weren't the only chores connected with making the boxes—the thin strips of poplar had to be cut into tiny pieces, each one only a fraction of an inch wide. The Shakers began weaving their first poplar boxes in the 1860s, and by 1872 they were still cutting poplar strips by hand; finally, in 1872, one of the brethren designed and built a machine to cut the strips quickly and easily.

After cutting, the next step was to weave the poplar strips together, and for that chore, the Shaker brethren built a special loom—one similar to looms used for weaving fabric. The tiny strips were woven together with sewing thread, and the woven material was cut off when it reached a length of approximately ten yards. Then began the final process of putting the boxes together. The material was ironed between two sheets of white paper to ensure that it was thoroughly dry and to make it stronger. Box sizes were already established, so the basketmakers knew exactly what size to cut each piece of material, and pieces of cardboard were cut to match, as the woven poplar needed reinforcement. The linings—velvet for jewelry boxes and satin for others—were glued to one side of the cardboard, and the woven poplar was glued to the other side. The edges were bound with thin strips of white leather, and the top was fastened on with satin ribbons.

In 1899 one of the sisters began using a few strands of sweet grass when making a poplar box. Nowhere have records been found indicating that Shaker boxes were ever made entirely of sweet grass. The woven-poplar boxes with the few strands of sweet grass were made for a few years, but they never gained the popularity of the boxes made entirely of woven poplar. Some believe this was due to the fact that sweet grass was associated with baskets made by the Indians, while the woven poplar was traditionally Shaker.

Sales of poplar boxes reached such proportions that the Shakers eventually published a catalogue picturing, describing, and pricing many of their boxes. When the *Catalogue of Fancy Goods* was published, customers had a choice of 32 items at prices ranging from 25 cents for a tray to $3.25, which would buy several types of boxes. Prices on the same boxes today range from around $75 to $300.

Shaker Copies

The most common practice in the world is for a person to copy something that has been or is successful. It was no different with the products of the Shakers. The Shaker basket business was considered very successful, and therefore basketmakers living in the areas of each community copied Shaker style and designs. For that reason it is now rather difficult to cull the copies from the real thing—and many people don't even try. They label anything that looks Shaker, "Shaker." In fact, an antique dealer offered this "gen-

Ash-splint basket after the Shaker style. 11" dia, 13" o.h. $50–$85

uine" Shaker basket from his private collection of Shaker baskets.

Shaker Picnic Basket

The imported willow picnic basket has long been known as the "Shaker picnic basket." See "Willow, Picnic Basket."

Shaving Horse

The *shaving horse,* used to split and smooth ash splints, resembles the harness maker's horse (the upright wooden contraption used to hold leather tautly while it is sewn). Shaving horses were handmade, and probably fashioned to the user's specifications. The shaving horse, also called a *drawing horse,* was used to hold poplar and ash splints in order to shave them thinner and make them smoother.

195

Shaving horse. $35–$60

Shelf Baskets or Trays

Shallow square and oblong trays were made to be used in presses, cupboards, and armoires. There were no closets as such, and no paper boxes in which to store clothing,

Shelf tray of woven, dyed oak splints. **$90–$125**

so the people used shallow baskets and trays that had lids to keep out dust and rodents.

Ship, Basketry

Novelties have long been made in basketry, but chances are sailing ships are among the more unusual items. No history is known about this item except that it was made in Portugal—recently. It was a souvenir item, no doubt. It is large and therefore difficult to display, and it catches dust that is hard to remove. The 22-inch-tall sails are held in place by palm-covered wires.

Basketry sailing ship. 12" w, 25" l, 22" h. $16–$35

Shipping Basket

The owner of this basket called it a shipping basket, but could give no reason for the name except that he felt the reinforcement strips on either side and the heavy splints made it a perfect basket for shipping. The splints are made of an unknown wood, but they are very attractive with the dark centers and light borders. More research is needed on this one.

So-called shipping basket. 13" w, 19" l, 10" h. $20–$30

Shoe Basket

An English writer called this English basket a "shoe basket," but went on to explain she thought the name referred more to the shape than to the use. It was actually used as an egg basket, she said. It is very much like our gizzard or buttocks baskets, although not nearly as deep. Like the American version, these egg baskets were made in a variety of sizes, and this example is one of the smaller ones. This one also has a twisted handle, whereas the American version has a strong splint handle.

Shopping Bags, Woven

Every basketmaker worthy of the name has at one time or another made a bag or basket to be used for general shopping. There seems to have been a tendency among all basketmakers to make deep round or square baskets for grocery shopping, and smaller oblong ones for general shopping.

After marketing, ladies had their afternoons free to go back into town to buy little things they needed, such as small pieces of lace and ribbon, or embroidery threads. A small basket was fine for this type of shopping. Later on, purchases were wrapped in paper and tied with a string, but they would have been difficult to carry without a shopping basket.

Open shopping bag woven of river cane by southern Indians. 6" w, 13" l, 14" o.h. $35–$59

Shoe basket. 9" dia, 8" o.h. $75–$90

Covered storage basket of a much later period, triple-woven cane. 14" w, 24" l, 7" h. $25–$45

Ash-splint, sweet-grass, and Hong Kong grass shopping bag. 7" w, 14½" l, 16" o.h. $29–$45

Ash-splint shopping basket, Passamaquoddy. 5¾" w, 16" l, 18" o.h. $35–$55

Sieve, Horsehair

Around 1885, the Shakers at Sabbathday Lake revived an old craft, that of making small sieves using horsehair. It remained one of their major crafts for nearly 40 years. The majority of the sieves were miniatures, that is, $2\frac{1}{2}$ to $3\frac{1}{2}$ inches in diameter, and they were set in maple frames.

Sieves are not really a part of the basketry scene, yet the bottoms must always be woven in an over-and-under design, like woven baskets.

A century or so ago, when horses were so plentiful, the hair from their manes and tails was used in many ways. It was used to make bottoms for sieves, handles for basketry water jugs, and jewelry. A few Indians still make horsehair baskets and a little jewelry.

This sieve is larger than those known to have been made by the Shakers, and it has a pine frame rather than a maple frame, but it is constructed exactly like those made by them.

Horsehair sieve. 8" dia, 4" h. $125–$185

Sifter

When and where this sifter was made is unknown, but the workmanship is absolutely superb. Unlike most sifters that have splints fastened around the bottom, this one has them fastened into points on the sides. It may have been used for winnowing grain or rice, but more than likely it was used to sift meal before making cornbread. Other sifters were made plain with a splint bottom.

Plain sifter with pine band. 16" dia, 4½" h. $100–$150

Fancy sifter with splints fastened on the sides. 18" dia, 4½" h. $125–175

Singeing Baskets

It's nearly impossible to remove all of the superficial hairlike threads on baskets made from oak, hickory, and elm splints, unless the hairs are singed lightly. If they're singed for too long, or too much, the fire will, of course, burn the splints. A light singeing will remove all the stray hairs or threads.

Single-Wrapped Rims

Concern about the wrapping on the top and rim of a basket is limited almost exclusively to splint baskets. A coil basket doesn't have

Basket with single-wrapped rim and notched handle.

that type of rim, but it does have to be secured well, as do all baskets. Single-wrapped is not as strong or as sturdy as double-wrapped and may not last as long. Single-wrapped means the splint was wrapped around the rim once and no more.

Skep

Another name for beehives made of coiled rye grass. See "Beehives."

Skye Hen Basket

This was the name given broody hen baskets made by the basketmakers of Kilmuir Skye. See "Hen Basket."

Smilax

Smilax has long been a favorite vine for decorations, especially at Southern weddings. Smilax has also been used to make baskets. When the roughness is removed from the vines, they make strong, flexible spokes and weavers for baskets.

Soloman's Seal

The berries of this plant (*Polygonatum biflorum*) were used by the New England basketmakers to make red dye for their basket materials. It's a perennial plant with bell-shaped flowers and dark-red berries. The name is believed to come from the markings on the roots. See "Red" under "Dyes."

Sorghum or Sugar Cane Leaves

There is hardly a material on earth that can be coiled, woven, or twined that hasn't been used to make baskets. Corn shucks have been used, as have the long leaves or "fodder" from the cane stalks. This is a coarse material and it didn't make pretty baskets, according to some, but it was sometimes used for that purpose. It has been described as very ornamental by some old basketmakers who liked the beautiful colors and coarse texture. The colors are beautiful in the fall, when they begin to turn from yellows to oranges and on to reds. Some turn a violet color, while others turn brown. By using the leaves while the colors are changing it is possible to make a variegated basket that is as pretty as a dyed basket. The leaves have to be coiled like those used in pine needle baskets.

Sotol

Sotol refers to any number of related tree-like plants growing in the deserts of the Southwest. They also grow in northern Mexico. The plant has clusters of whitish, lilylike flowers and leaves that can be split into small quarter-inch strips and used in making twilled baskets. Sharp, thorny teethlike growths on the leaves have to be removed before they can be used.

Souvenir Baskets, Contemporary

As with basketmakers in the past, basketmakers today must depend to a great extent

Colorful, covered basket made of palm leaves. 10" w, 16" l, 11½" h. $8–$20

on the tourist trade to sell their baskets. Some of the most colorful tourist-trade baskets are being made in Haiti and the surrounding islands (just as they have been for a long time). They are made of palm leaves that have been dyed bright colors.

Sowing Baskets

There were sowing baskets just as there were sewing baskets. The latter was used in the house to keep sewing needs, while the former might be fastened around the waist, draped over the shoulder, or carried in the hand. The sowing basket was filled with seeds that could be dropped in hills or broadcast over fields.

In some areas, oak-splint baskets like this were used for sowing. 7" w, 12" l, 11" o.h. $25–$39

Spokes

Spokes are the splints used to form the bottom of a woven basket; they're continued up to where the sides of the basket will be, forming a foundation for later weaving. Spokes have to be strong if the basket is going to be sturdy and durable. In most baskets, the spokes are a bit heavier than the splints used as weavers. Also called *standards*.

Spruce Roots

In early writings, this tree was referred to as *spruse*, and even then the use of spruce roots for sewing baskets together, especially birch-bark baskets and boxes, was discussed. In fact, spruce roots are as important to some basketmakers as oak splints are to others.

Sitka spruce, grown in areas of Alaska and California, was very important to basketmakers, who boiled the roots and then split them to make a coarse foundation splint. Black, white, and red spruce grow best in the northern part of the country, and all three have tough, flexible roots that are excellent for use in basketry. Spruce roots were almost indispensable for making birch-bark containers; they were needed to sew the boxes together. Small roots, excellent for sewing birch-bark pieces, could usually be found around the younger trees, but if it was not available, the worker could peel and scrape the roots down to the needed size. It also could be split for finer sewing.

Square Bottom and Round Top

Basketmakers used to say that making a basket with a square bottom and a round top required lots of skill. But making the bonnet basket pictured shouldn't have been that difficult; the maker put a solid wooden

Rim of square basket showing how the round top was made.

rim around the top, forcing it into the desired size and shape.

Squaw Grass

Squaw grass is another name for golden ragwort. It grows all over America, mostly in moist meadows and swamps, and is used in basketry. See "Golden Ragwort."

Star Design

The star was a favorite design with Indian basketmakers of the Southwest. Some stars were left plain, while others were outlined in a different color. It is impossible to date most baskets, but this one appears to be 25 years old or older. It is a coiled basket whose bright colors haven't faded too much.

Collared bowl-type basket. 8¼" dia, 5" h. $24–$35

Stationery Basket

It has been said that when the Indians of Maine discovered tourists, they found them to be one of their best natural resources. For a century or more, tourists flocked to Maine to spend their summers. As was the vacationing custom in those days, the entire family spent the summer at a spa or favorite

Ash-splint and sweet-grass stationery basket; Unity College collection. $35–$47

resort hotel, usually on the coast. Not only did they have the entire coast, they also had places like Bar Harbor, Old Orchard, and Poland Spring. Families came bringing their maids, governesses, and coachmen. Horse and carriage arrived on the same train as the family and servants, and quarters were provided for both servants and horses.

It didn't take long for the basketmakers—whites, Indians, and Shakers—to discover the lucrative tourist market. Before, basketmakers made mostly utilitarian baskets, but suddenly they began making what they previously would have considered to be frivolous—things like stationery baskets.

The tourists of that day were a letter-writing crowd—people wrote to their friends rather than calling them on the telephone. Correspondence was heavy, and postage was only a penny for a postcard and 2 cents for a letter. A stationery basket was very handy for holding incoming and outgoing mail.

202

Stitched-grass basket. 6" dia, 3" h, 9" o.h. **$15–$20**

Stitched-Grass Basket

It is not known when or where these stitched-grass baskets were made. They're not very attractive, and, apparently, few were made, because not many are seen now. The stitched-grass basket shown in the photograph is an unusual one. The lid was made to fit over the handle and cannot be removed; it can only be raised and lowered.

Storage or Utility Baskets

Ask a dozen oldtimers how storage baskets were used, and you'll probably get a dozen different answers. Apparently, they were used for whatever the owner needed them for at the moment. Some say they were used as feather baskets; others say they were used to store feather beds in the summer when it was too hot to sleep on them. No doubt, they were also used for clothing storage and possibly for household linens.

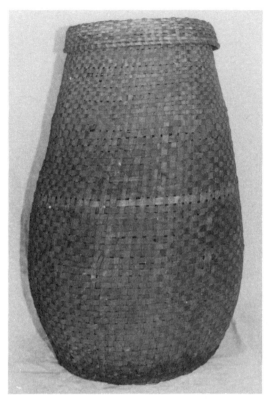

Plain ash-splint storage basket. 14" dia, 30" h. **$150–$175**

Fancy ash-splint storage basket with dyed, but badly faded weavers. 19" dia, 28" h. **$175–$250**

Open Cherokee-made cane storage basket.
$500–$750

Notice how fragile-looking the handles are, especially for use on something as large as a storage basket. The plain storage basket doesn't even have handles.

Strawberry-Picking Baskets

This is a primitive strawberry-picking basket and is used here to complete the basketry picture. The wooden carrier was handmade—but not woven, coiled, or twined—and it was built to hold eight factory-made quart baskets (the poorly made dispensable type that could be filled with

Strawberry-picking basket with two factory-made quart-size containers. 26" l, 11½" o.h. $10–$20

berries and then sold without changing the berries from one container to another). In many strawberry-growing areas, strawberry-picking baskets are being phased out and are slowly finding their way into antique shops, shows, and malls.

Strawberry-Shaped Basket

The Passamaquoddy Indians of Maine were the first to make the various baskets shaped like fruits and nuts. Using ash splints and red dye, they concocted a strawberry-shaped basket similar to the acorn basket. It is shaped like a strawberry, with red curliques around the side and green leaves on the top for a very realistic look.

Strawberry-shaped basket made of ash splints (dyed red and green) and sweet grass. 5" dia, 3½" h. New, $20–$35; old, $25–$40

Straw-and-Skin Dryer

The only feature of this contraption that would remotely connect it with basketry is the coiled straw sides. This is truly basketry in its most primitive form. Origin and use are unknown, but the dealer who sold it thought it might have been used for drying something like seed or wool. The outside is made of sheep skin, and some primitively cured, small pieces of wool are still attached. Five coils of wrapped straw were placed inside to keep the bottom taut and

Straw-and-skin dryer. 15" dia, 3½" h. $30–$40

the sides standing; otherwise, it would collapse.

String Holder

The majority of old string holders were made of either wood or iron, but there were a few made of basketry materials. Some were made

String holder open showing the two sections.

Rattan string holder. 6½" dia, 5" h. $35–$45

to resemble beehives—flat on the bottom and rounded at the top, with a hole in the top for thread to come through. Later string holders were made of rattan on a plywood base. The wood and iron string holders were mostly used in grocery and department stores; before the introduction of paper and plastic bags, string was needed to wrap packages. A large number of ash-splint and sweet-grass string holders were made in the Northeast and sold to tourists for use in the home.

Sumac

Sumac was one of the most useful plants in basketmaking, with the exception of various splints and pine needles. The stalk was used in making basket foundations, and also yellow dye was obtained from it. The slender branches of the low-growing sumac were used by Indians more than any other rod material, except for willow. By simply putting the peeled sumac branches in water filled with berry stems from the alder, the branches were easily dyed to make dark weavers. Sumac is a versatile plant: The powdered leaves from some species are used for tanning and dyes, while other species are used in medicine.

Sumitori Kago

Sumitori kago is the Japanese name for the basket that was used for holding brazier charcoal in homes. In earlier days, a *brazier* was used to heat each room of the house, and a container was necessary to keep a supply of charcoal on hand. Although these baskets were not often seen, the workmanship on the sumitori kago was as excellent as that on the finest basket.

Swastika Design

Long before Hitler adopted the swastika as his own, it was considered to be a good luck symbol. It has a long history and has been

Coiled basket with swastika design. 4" dia, 3" h. $200–$300, depending on size.

found in ancient Rome, in excavations of Grecian cities, on Buddhist idols, and on Chinese coins dated as early as 315 B.C. The Indians of the Southwest have always used it, on amulets and as decoration for their baskets. To them it was a charm that would drive away evil and bring good luck. The Apaches are credited with using the symbol more than anyone else. The settlers also considered the swastika to be a charm; they believed that it was formed from four *L*s, representing *light, love, luck,* and *life.*

The arms of the swastika can bend to the left or the right. And they can vary, even on the same basket. The photograph provides a prime example. One swastika is 1¾ inches, while the largest is 3 inches.

Sweet Grass

Sweet grass is the common name given to one of the eight species of grass grown from Newfoundland to Alaska, then southward to New Jersey and westward to Colorado. *Hierochole odorata* is the botanical name.

Once upon a time sweet grass was sold by the bunch in northern Europe where it was hung in bedrooms on the assumption that it induced sleep. The Europeans also used it in religious festivities. They spread it in front of their churches and placed it along the paths to shrines (which is why it became known as holy grass). In ancient

Scotland there was a marriage rite called "handfasting" in which the bride and groom sat before their friends with his right hand tied to her left. The material used to tie their hands was none other than sweet grass.

Excavations in the northeastern sections of the United States indicate that the Indians in the area have used sweet grass as long or longer than the Europeans. At one time some Indian men made a living gathering sweet grass and selling it to basketmakers.

Sweet Vernal Grass

Sweet vernal grass is the correct name, but in many places it is called *sweet grass* by those who use it in basketry. Growing abundantly in both England and the eastern part of the United States, it is a sweet-scented grass that gives the surrounding area a marvelous, light-scented fragrance—hence, its name. The fragrance of sweet grass lingers for years after it has been woven or coiled into a basket. See "Sweet Grass."

Much sweet grass was used in the Passamaquoddy-made baskets. $29–$45

Sweetzer Baskets

The Sweetzer family has been making baskets in Waterbury, Vermont, for more than 125 years. Unlike so many old basketmaking families today, the fourth generation of this family continues to make the same type baskets as those of their earlier generations, and they still use ash splints.

Swing-Handle Baskets

Swing-handle baskets, are the most sought after of the old woven-splint baskets. Basketmakers have always made swing handles—usually on burden or work baskets—and through the years, many of the handles have simply worn out. It's difficult to attribute swing handles—or, as they are

Poor replica of the Nantucket basket; the swing-handle is fastened with brass screws $100–$150

Desirable swing-handle basket, self-fastened.

Hairpin-loop, fastened swing-handle basket.

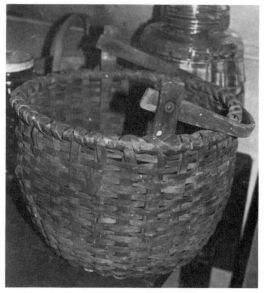

Old basket with crudely attached swing-handle. $150–$200

*Swing-handle baskets are among the most expensive today. The handles were attached in various ways. This one works on a loop. Baskets of this type sell in the **$400–$600** range.*

*Swing handle fastened on reinforced loop. **$350–$550***

*Taconic (Taghkanic) swing handles were attached this way. **$400–$600***

*Top has been repaired with twine. Good swing handle. Damaged, **$100–$150**.*

*Half-bushel oak-splint basket with swing handle and double-wrapped top. **$400–$550***

sometimes called, *drop handles*—to any one maker, with the exception of the Taghkanic or Bushwhacker baskets, the Nantucket Lightship basket, and the new ones being made today. Many of the skilled basketmakers today are making swing handles because they're more sought after and higher priced. It is not unusual to find new, well-made swing handle baskets priced in the $500-and-up bracket.

A swing-handle basket is classified as such when the handle is free swinging; that is, it will fall to either side, allowing the basket to be filled without interference from the handle (but the handle can be raised when needed).

Not all swing-handles were beautifully made. Some were simply bolted onto a wooden splint or ear that rose above the top of the basket. There are all kinds of swing-handle baskets, but the most expensive and sought after is the kind having a loop or hole at the end of the handle that fits into a loop or hole made at the top of the basket.

Swing-Handle Basket, New

One of the most intriguing new baskets seen recently is the oak-splint swing-handle basket pictured, which is stamped on the bottom "Made in China for Basketville." (Basketville is a 150-year-old basket factory in Putney, Vermont.) The basket is absolutely beautiful—it is the type collectors will be fighting over in 75 or 100 years.

The mystery of why a basket factory would import baskets is explained on the attached label. It is a joint venture, with the ash or oak splints being cut in Vermont and shipped to China, where the baskets are handmade before they are shipped back to Vermont.

Information on the other side of the label explains that the basket is "an authentic reproduction of an early New England basket. Handwoven in the Shaker style and

destined to become tomorrow's heirloom." The weaving resembles the Shaker style, but if the Shakers made swing-handle baskets, no record of them has been found. They may have made a few for their own use.

Taconic Baskets

Also known as Bushwhacker baskets, these baskets were made for well over a century by a group living in the New York village of Taghkanic, now simplified to Taconic. See "Bushwhacker Baskets."

Tall-Handled Baskets

For a basketmaker making baskets long ago, the task was somewhat like that of an experienced cook experimenting with various

New swing-handle basket made of oak splints. 10" dia, 13" o.h. $30–$35

Tall-handled ash-splint basket. 4½" w, 9½" l, 21" o.h. $23–$30

Crudely cut splints, what appears to be some kind of cord weavers, and a tall, vine handle make up this basket. 6" sq, 18" o.h. $10–$19

Cane and willow shopping basket. 8" w, 12" l, 10½" h. $17–$35

dishes. The cook wanted to try something new—maybe a new combination. Basketmakers did the same thing: They made whatever they liked, wanted, or needed. No explanation has been found as to why basketmakers made such tall handles on some of the baskets, unless it was to accommodate long-stemmed flowers.

Tall, Oval Shopping Basket

The question often arises among basket collectors as to how much the weaving method can be changed. The method can be changed very little, but the types of baskets can vary considerably.

That point is further proved by a book published in England in 1959. It is interesting to see how many of that country's baskets are similar to American baskets and how many are different. Materials can differ; for example, instructions for a carpet beater suggested using cane or "palembang." Apparently, that is a cane from a specific area, as Palembang is the trade center and river port of southeastern Sumatra, Indonesia.

Illustrations and directions were given in the English book for making a tall oval shopping basket. The basket could be made of cane, but buff willow would give color and strength, the author said. The size of the finished basket given in the book is exactly the same as the one pictured, which suggests that the one pictured was made in England or by English directions.

Tamarack

Also known as *tamarack pine,* this tree is found along the Pacific coast, from California to Alaska. Other species are found in swamps and cooler places. Tamarack roots were used by some of the older Indians in their basketry.

Tarahumara Indians

By the boundaries established today, the Tarahumaras would be considered Mexican Indians; however, in the early days, they ignored boundaries—except when the boundaries concerned another's hunting grounds.

The area inhabited by the Tarahumaras was a rugged, arid area that didn't encourage agriculture. For that reason, the Tarahumaras developed a lifestyle much like that of the early basketmakers—a simple lifestyle that was mostly self-sufficient. Living this somewhat isolated existence in the mountainous country of northern Mexico, the Tarahumaras experienced many hardships through the years and were faced with poverty and near starvation at times.

Small Tarahumara basket of palm fiber. $2\frac{1}{2}$" dia, 4" h. $10–$20

Only recently have they acquired plastic containers to replace the baskets they made and used throughout the centuries. They had long been making lidded baskets, called *piticas*, which were usually made of twilled bear grass. Like so many others at that time, they used baskets to store their possessions.

There was a time when every Tarahumara woman made baskets, but today it's difficult to find many of the beautiful, double-woven, lidded piticas. They still make a few single-weave baskets, but most of them are only 1 to 4 inches tall.

Tatting Basket

Tatting was fancy stitchery work enjoyed by many ladies over the years. It was tedious work, but the ladies could take it with them when visiting neighbors or traveling by train, or they could tat as they sat around on the porches of resort hotels during the summer. Nearly every lady did some sort of fancy needlework in those days—it was like the badge of a good homemaker. Naturally, the ladies were delighted with the small tatting baskets they could carry on their arms—baskets that would hold their tatting shuttle and thread.

Fancy ash-splint and cord tatting basket. $4\frac{1}{2}$" dia, $5\frac{1}{2}$" h. $20–$35

Tea Basket

Baskets have always been named for the purposes for which they were used. In some

211

Rattan tea basket. 11" w, 16" l, 6" h. $25–$45

cases the name has lasted longer than the basket, while in other cases the name has changed with usage or with the language. No record has been found for the original name or use for this Oriental-made rattan basket. In America we would probably call it a picnic basket, but the English lady who owned it called it a tea basket.

Tea Cozy

In the Roaring Twenties, women in New York State, and maybe in other areas as well, referred to this as a *tea cozy*. It is almost identical to the teapot basket, but it has "Made in China" on the bottom of the teapot, whereas the Rose Medallion pot in the teapot basket (see "Teapot Basket") does not.

This same type of basket was made around 1930 when the fancy brass hardware was replaced with leather hinges and handles to make an unusual purse for an exclu-

Tea cozy. 8" w, 10½" l, 8" h. $88–$125

sive New York wholesaler of women's wear. The name of the shop and "handmade" was stamped on the leather lining.

The lining is red plaid and is insulated with a firm material. The weight of the cozy is 4 pounds.

Teapot Basket

There is hardly a home in New England that doesn't have a treasure trove of gifts brought from around the world. For centuries, men have sailed the seas and brought back gifts for family and friends. Baskets like the one in the photograph were brought back (and many were imported) to use during tea time. This basket contained a Rose Medallion teapot and was lined to protect it. The basket is made of reeds wrapped with what appears to be thinly cut bamboo. The handle and fasteners are brass. Some of the baskets also contain cups to match the teapot.

Lined basket with Rose Medallion teapot. 7" w, 10" l, 6¾" h. $100–$175

Teienametakwatha

Mohawk name for the knee vice or separator. See "Knee Vise."

Thimble Baskets

Indians of the Northeast made thimble cases or baskets of sweet grass and thin ash splints specifically for the tourist trade. Thimble baskets made excellent souvenirs and gifts, because at that time everybody was sewing and needed a thimble, from the housewife who was responsible for the family clothing and linens to the young girl learning her stitches. Thimbles were so important they were included on the chatelaine (see "Chatelaine").

With the increased interest in all things basketry, thimble baskets are again being made by some of the Indians in the Northeast. There is a scarcity of good ash to make splints, so the basketmakers are probably delighted to have a use for the scrap pieces left over from larger baskets. The ash splints for the thimble baskets are cut $\frac{1}{16}$ of an inch wide and only need to be a few inches long. The sweet grass is then woven over the splints.

Sweet-grass and ash-splint thimble case or basket. 1" dia, 1" h. $6–$23

Thompson River Indians

The name was derived from their location, the Thompson River, in Canada. Also called Thompson Indians. They were noted for their excellent baskets made with bold geometric designs.

Tobacco Baskets

In places like Tennessee and Kentucky, where tobacco is grown, cut, dried, and then carried to the tobacco auctions, farmers use a flat basket contraption that more closely resembles the lid from a large basket than anything else. Called simply a *tobacco basket,* this type of basket is beginning to show up in antique shops around the country. It is large, approximately 40 × 40 inches, and is factory-made using loosely woven 6-inch splints. Some antique dealers say there is now a big demand for these baskets among younger people who use them for wall decorations. More surprisingly than their popularity are the prices they're bringing. In New England, the going price is $33 to $55 each.

Torchère

In one of the 1925 books on instructions for making basketry items, a torchère is shown, but no instructions are given. The dictionary describes a torchère as a small, high candlestick, and that is exactly what is pictured. It appears to be about 2 feet tall, with a base that closely resembles a small wicker lamp. It has a tall, slim shade, and the entire piece is decorated with wooden beads (that is, the beads were woven in as the piece was made). A candle is placed inside through the top and lighted from the top.

Tufted Hair Grass

This is one of the many grasses used in basketry. It is most likely found in one of three places: rich soil in drained fields, clay woodlands, and on the banks of rivers and streams. When sheltered by trees, it becomes very luxuriant. Tufted hair grass has strong, stiff stems that grow as high as two and three feet. It grows extremely well in the mountains of New Mexico, and in California, where the split stems are used to make a white design in split-root baskets.

Tule

Tule can best be described as a kind of large bullrush. It is found in marshy places in the West and Southwest and is used extensively in basketry. In fact, tule can be used in a number of ways. The slender roots of the plant can be dried and used for twining a red design in weaving, and the stems can be split or left whole for use in large baskets. The section between the roots and stem is the most valuable of all: The bark can be split from this section and used to make mats, and the outside of the stems can be split into very narrow strips, then twisted into thin threads for use in making twined baskets.

Tumpline

A *tumpline* is a carrying strap that was fastened on a basket and then put across the carrier's head in order to carry heavy burden baskets. Some tribes made skull-cap type hats to protect their heads against the weight of tumplines. Since many Indian families moved frequently during those early years, it was necessary to move their food and, in some cases, their lodging. They had no other means of transporting their possessions than by canoe, sled, or basket and tumpline. By using a tumpline, a man or woman could carry from 100 to 150 pounds with ease.

Umbrella Stand

During the Victorian era when the popularity of basketry was at its peak, the umbrella or *parasol* was an essential. Parasols weren't merely for rainy days—they were for any trips outside the house. Ladies of the day tried to avoid the sun as much as possible, because a pale complexion was desirable.

To accommodate the number of umbrellas in a home, umbrella stands were either bought or made. Some homes used hall trees along with umbrella stands, and the most popular stands were made like baskets. These were made in a variety of shapes and sizes, but most were made of wooden splints or willow.

Unfinished Basketry

Unfinished pieces of basketry have few uses, other than for study. In the Unity College basket display, unfinished baskets are used to show the steps in basketmaking. Oftentimes, pieces are found that can be finished, and, if that's not feasible, the pieces of old

A pair of unfinished ash-splint and Hong Kong grass vases.

Two unfinished baskets in the Unity College display.

214

splint can be used to repair broken baskets. Such splints may have aged enough to match those found on old baskets.

Uses for Baskets

As always, baskets can be used for storing and carrying various items, but there are dozens of other uses as well.

Baskets can be lined with aluminum foil to make containers for small flowering plants; new or damaged baskets are best for this job. A basket of fruit or nuts makes a nice gift for a sick friend or shut-in, and a basket filled with talcum, soap, lotion, and a nice bathcloth or hand towel makes a welcome gift for someone in the hospital. Try a different approach to gift-giving and send a basket sometime, rather than flowers.

Small baskets can be used in numerous ways around the house, which allows one to show off a collection of baskets while keeping them useful. Baskets make great napkin or flatware holders for picnic tables, and they make excellent holders for mail and cosmetics.

One of the most enjoyable ways to use small covered baskets (new ones will work just as well as old) is for saving flower petals. Place the petals in a basket and add a few drops of your favorite perfume—the fragrance will linger for weeks. More perfume added at intervals revives the fragrance.

Vanilla Grass

No explanation other than the fragrance can be found for giving the name *vanilla grass* to sweet grass. Sweet grass has a very pleasant odor that lasts for years and can be revived by simply wetting a sweet-grass basketry piece periodically.

Vases With Basketry Covers

Basketmakers of the Northeast have been weaving covers on vases for nearly a cen-

African violet in a basket.

Basketry-covered clear vase. 6" dia, 10" h. $15–$25

215

Basketry-covered vase. 6" dia, 9" h. $16–$29

tury, and it's amazing how they're able to recognize each other's work still—their later work, that is.

The vase with the small top (above) was found at a yard sale in Portland, Maine. Later, at a basketry class conducted on the Penobscot Indian Reservation in Old Town, Maine, approximately 100 miles away, the vase was shown to the instructor—an older, very skilled Penobscot basketmaker. She immediately recognized the work as that of her sister-in-law from the 1930s. The cover is woven of thin strips of ash mixed with Hong Kong grass and sweet grass. The strips were originally dyed in shades of red and blue, but are now faded. The scalloped top of a red Depression-glass vase can be seen at the top. The other vase pictured is clear and is about the same age, and the basketry cover is about the same.

Vietnamese Baskets

Once basketmakers learn their craft, it isn't easy to change. The displaced Vietnamese coming into the United States are not changing their style of basketry as much as they're having to change the types of materials they use. They must either substitute their usual materials with American-grown cane, or try to have materials imported from home. Not all Vietnamese are making baskets here, but several are making them to be sold in gift shops. The Vietnamese-made baskets that were seen were well made and very attractive.

New Vietnamese basket. 4" w, 6" l, 10" o.h. $15–$25

Virginia Creeper

Virginia creeper, a vine, was used rather extensively in baskets about a century ago. It is also called *American ivy* and *five-leaf ivy* in some areas.

The most desirable runners, at that time, were those that grew close to the ground. The runners are brown and a bit rough, which gives the basket an almost antique appearance when new.

Virgina creeper is also called *woodbine,* and is sometimes mistaken for poison ivy. However, it has a five-part leaf, and poison ivy has only a three-part leaf. At one time, Virginia creeper was a highly cultivated plant because it was so pretty when the foliage turned scarlet in the fall. It has a small, round, dark-blue berry (inedible), and it grows in the woods from Quebec to Florida, and around Texas and Mexico.

Wall Baskets

Wall baskets were made by most basketmakers in all areas, for both their own use

Single-pocket wall basket made of birch bark and decorated with porcupine quills. Quills on pocket are worn. 8" w, 7" h. $75–$105

Three-pocket, ash-splint wall basket. $135–$175

Chitimacha cane wall basket. $200–$250

217

Deep, single-pocket wall basket made of ash splint and decorated in the Penobscot manner. 8" w, 10" h. $75–$95

Oak-splint wall basket. $39–$60

and for sale. The baskets were used in a variety of ways, and their names often reflected their use. Wall baskets were used to hold knives and forks in some areas, combs and brushes in others, and in some places they were used to hold mail. In still other places they were filled with shuttles for the loom. Some had single pockets; others had two and three pockets. In the South, wall baskets were often made of swamp cane; in the East, ash splint; and in Tennessee, Kentucky, Missouri, Kansas, and other areas, they were made of oak splints.

Recent wall basket for flowers. 7½" dia, 14" h. $10–$18

Wallet

This is a simple envelope-type wallet made of woven grass, and little is known about it. It appears to date from around the 1920s or 1930s, and it is definitely souvenir-type basketry. This wallet resembles the palm-leaf purses made for women but appears to be of a finely cut grass. A two-row design is worked in, on both the inside and outside pieces, and the edge is beautifully finished.

Woven grass wallet with woven palm-leaf liner. 6" w, 4" h. $7–$10

Walnut

Lumber from the walnut tree has always been sought for making good furniture, but as far as is known, few, if any, walnut splints were used in basketry. The bark, however, was used for both splints and dye. Darker than the white oak splints often used with it, the inner bark of the walnut tree was split and used to make contrasting designs.

Wastebaskets

Wastebaskets are modern basketry items that weren't even known or used as such until around the turn of the twentieth century. Prior to that time, baskets were used for saving papers like receipts, letters, and bills, and they were used as plunder baskets— but they were not used for collecting trash.

Shortly after the turn of the century, imported Oriental baskets began to be used for holding excess or waste papers; thus, the wastebasket was born. In recent years, basketmakers have recognized the need for wastebaskets and have begun making them. At a showing of Coushatta Indian–made pine needle baskets a few years ago, there were five different sizes of wastebaskets on display.

New Choctaw cane wastebasket. 15" dia, 16" h. $50–$75

Water Jug, Basketry

In the arid Southwest the Indians had to have some means of carrying water from the stream or river to their home. There were no buckets, not even wooden ones, so they devised and made a watertight jug in

219

Water jug with broken horsehair handle; much of the resin has worn off. 6" dia, 6" h. $225–$275

basketry. The jugs were usually coiled using the two stacked rod method and when completed were rubbed with a mixture of ground cactus leaves and powdered juniper leaves. This mixture filled the spaces between the stitches and the coils. Next, resin from the piñon tree was poured into the jug, along with some heated stones to keep the resin soft until it could ooze into all the openings. The outside was brushed with the resin.

After traders opened the Southwest, many of the Indians discarded their water-jugs for containers the traders brought. But there was a large group who continued to use basketry water jugs into the 1930s. With the popularity of basketry increasing daily some of the tribes are again making water jugs, not to use but to sell to the tourists.

Waterproof Baskets

A couple of centuries ago—in some areas only a century ago—when there were no plastic containers or wooden buckets, ways had to be devised for carrying water from springs and creeks. This was especially true for the people of the arid sections of the Southwest.

The Apaches are credited with making the first woven water jugs—they were the most skilled basketmakers—but it's believed that the Paiutes made the best waterproof jugs. Their jugs were made of willow coated with gum from the piñon trees. The Havasupais are credited with making the first stand-up basketry water jugs—those with pointed bottoms made for standing in the ground. The Cherokees also made waterproof baskets of double-woven river cane coated with beeswax.

Weavers

Whether they're made of wood splints, swamp cane, or bamboo, the pieces used in over and under weaving around the sides of a woven basket are called weavers. Even the braided and plaited sweet grass used with ash splints are called weavers when used to weave the sides of a basket.

Wedge

The wedge is another tool necessary in the preparation of splint basketry materials, especially oak, elm, and hickory splints. The wedge is inserted into logs or sections of a tree, and when it is hit with a maul, it breaks the sections apart.

Weirs

Building weirs started with the early settlers, probably the Indians, and then spread across the country. The weirs were made of willow using the basketry technique of over-and-under weaving and placed in a pond or stream to catch fish.

Western Apache Indians

Trying to establish the age of any basket can be as tricky as trying to determine the maker, but the average collector says that establishing the age of a basket made in the Southwest, unless one is a student of that phase of basketry, is the most difficult. And there are those who say that dating a basket made by the Western Apache is the hardest of all.

The Western Apache were well known for their water jugs and their burden baskets, which were made in several sizes and shapes. They also made a variety of coiled jars, or *ollas*. They seemed to have used many varied designs, perhaps more than some other tribes used. The diamond design was a favorite, as was the cross, the swastika, chevrons, and coyote tracks. Occasionally they may have woven in a date or initial in a letter of the English alphabet, but there is some doubt as to whether such an instance was really an initial or was perhaps just a design (the letters used were *P, T, F,* and *H.*

Thirteen-inch tray similar to those made by the Western Apache Indians. $440–$750

Wheat Stitch

This fancy stitch was and still is used quite often in coil basketry. This stitch is believed to make the baskets more attractive, especially the pine needle baskets, and therefore it is used extensively throughout the South.

New pine needle and raffia tray in wheat stitch. 9" w, 12" l. $35–$55

Wheat-Straw Basket

Nearly everything that grows in the fields and forest has, at one time or another, been used in basketry. The basket pictured is another example of human ingenuity. The coiled basket is made of wheat straw and fastened with strips or splints that appear to be some kind of bark.

Wheat-straw basket. 8" dia, 4" h. $20–$29

Wheel Covers

When a carriage or wagon was used to transport the family to church on Sunday, or when a lady traveled any place, she wore long, billowing dresses with at least a half dozen ruffled petticoats, and sometimes she would wear a hoop skirt. Whether she was wearing a hoop skirt or petticoat, entering or leaving the carriage was difficult. This was especially true during winter and on rainy days.

Most ladies had very few pieces of clothing, and took very good care of what they did have. Eventually, woven wheel covers were invented, which served to cover the mud as passengers entered and left their vehicles. Later, wheel covers were offered in catalogues as "French wicker wheel covers and dress guards."

Some of these covers were destroyed when they were on the wheels, and others were discarded when they were no longer needed, and were eventually destroyed. Those that weren't destroyed simply rotted away in the weather. They are scarce now and cost in the $250 bracket when found.

Wickerwork

Many baskets are described as wicker baskets, yet the dictionary describes wickerwork as "thin, flexible twigs woven together."

Actually, *wickerwork* means that the *spokes,* or vertical part of a basket, is more rigid than the weavers. To further confuse the issue, some of the old basketry instruction books referred to a number of weaves as *wicker weaves.* These included the simple over-and-under weave and the double over-and-under weave, where two weavers were used as one. There was also a triple weave.

Old basketmakers used dozens of different weaves, including one called a *Japanese weave,* in which a single weaver was passed in front of two spokes and behind a third, using three spokes in one weave. This was often called *wickerwork.*

Willow wickerwork carrying basket with cover. 14" w, 17" l, 19" o.h. $75–$100

Wicopy

Wicopy is a modernization of the old term *kakisooikbe,* used by the Penobscots for a century or more to describe their ash-splint basket materials. It has also been called *wigobi.* All three terms were used to describe the flexibility of ash splints, which can be twisted and turned in various ways without breaking.

Willow

Through the years, willow trees have served us well. In earlier years, willow trees were unequaled for holding unruly streams. More useful, perhaps, were the branches or *osiers* used for making wiers, cradles, baskets, and, finally, wicker furniture.

Despite its many uses, willow was not cultivated during the early years; instead, it was allowed to grow wherever plants sprouted—unless they interfered with housebuilding, gardening, or farming. Then, with the popularity of wicker furniture shortly

Old willow basket with crisscross handles on the sides. 12" dia, 9½" h. $60–$90

Willow basket with coats of white paint on the bottom and red paint around the sides. 16" dia, 5" h. $25–$40

Willow basket that may be part of a nesting set. 14" dia, 4" h. $30–$50

before the turn of the century, Americans began to see the value of growing and harvesting willow holts.

Prior to that time, most willow had been imported from England, Belgium, Holland, and Germany, with Germany being the leader with a reported 50,000 acres of willows planted in 1898.

At about the same time, wicker furniture production and willow basketry began to skyrocket. The need for domestic willow became apparent, and so the Department of Agriculture began to educate the farmers in the ways of growing willow for profit. Free instructions were offered for planting, growing, and harvesting willow, and different varieties were recommended for certain areas.

Green willow was highly recommended for the southern states of Alabama, Mississippi, and Louisiana, and for some of the northern states. Purple willow was recommended for any area where willow would grow, and was one of the best varieties of willow around. It could be planted in rows, making it easier to cultivate with horse-drawn plows. Lemley willow was especially recommended for planting in Ohio, Indiana, and Maryland, but could be grown any place. It was least likely to become diseased, and therefore was most highly recommended. The willow holts grew fast and sold for good money, but there was still enough left over for basketmakers.

Due to its lightness and strength, willow is accorded a distinct place in the history of basketry. It has been used since the beginning of time. The Romans are known to have used willow for making baskets and beehives, as well as fences for their gardens. For years in Europe, willow was held in such high esteem that even in Pliny's time, he wrote, "Cato held an osier bed in higher estimation than an olive plantation or than wheat or meadow land."

The beauty of willow was not overlooked then, nor is it now. The white satiny smoothness of it's new branches gives it added appeal, while the brown of aged baskets gives it an added dimension. Willow baskets were so attractive that bakers once used them in their windows for displaying their finest pastries.

Not all willow branches were used in the sizes gathered from the tree. Many chose large branches or osiers for certain baskets, and smaller ones for other sizes. There were also the basketmakers, some Indian tribes among them, who opted for splitting willow branches into three pieces for very fine weaving. To split them, the branches were first soaked well, and then cut diagonally across one end. Using the Indian method of hands and teeth, the branch was divided into three parts by keeping one part between the teeth and holding the other two parts in each hand. The branch was pulled downward and outward until it came apart.

Willow Basketry Items

Willow Hot Pad

This hot pad is made of the same material and in the same design as the cover and base of the picnic hampers sold by the Shakers, who had supposedly imported them from Germany. There is no question that the Shakers sold the baskets both in their stores and on their delivery routes, but it is questionable whether the baskets came from Germany or the Orient.

Willow hot pad. 7½" w, 10" l. $10–$18

The same material and design was used in the sewing baskets and wine cradles. The weavers around the pad are so thin it would

have required a basketmaker with a lot of patience. The ripple effect is done by placing two small willow branches at regular intervals and then weaving over them.

Willow Picnic Baskets or Hampers

Controversy has surrounded these baskets for years, and all of it hasn't been cleared up yet. It probably began with a display of these baskets along with a large collection of Shaker-made baskets at a Shaker museum. Nobody asked questions, and everyone simply attributed the hampers to the Shakers. The curator was unable to give any information except the fact that they were sold by the Shakers.

Willow hamper lined with paper. 7" w, 13" l, 12½" o.h. $75–$125

Willow picnic hamper with fabric handle and base. 8" w, 13" l, 11" o.h. Damaged, $45–$75; good condition, $64–$90.

Close-up of finework on cover.

Willow sewing basket, probably sold in Shaker stores. 5" w, 10" l, 5½" h. $38–$65

Close-up of inside of basket.

Recently information came to light that these baskets were imported from Germany and sold in the Shaker stores but were not made by the Shakers. Prior to this time two wine cradles or baskets were found, made in the same style and of the same material. One has no identifying mark, but the other has "Indo China" stamped on the bottom. Clearly more research is needed in this category.

The hampers were made in at least two styles and in many sizes. One has a fabric-covered handle and base, indicating that it was probably covered in another, perhaps colorful, fabric; the Shakers very well could have made this addition. Judging by the ribbons on the woven poplar boxes, the Shakers loved to give items a personal, fancy touch.

Willow Sewing Basket

These willow sewing baskets are very similar, almost identical, to the hampers imported and sold in the Shaker stores. In fact, they probably could have been sold there also.

The small pockets or baskets on either end of the sewing basket raise some ques-

tions. They are made of grained-wood splints and a fabric or tape quite similar to that used by the Shakers to seat their chairs. The tape is now a solid beige color and is ⅜ inches wide. Willow was used throughout the basket, yet these pockets were attached with strong black thread, indicating that they might have been added later.

Willow Wine Cradles or Baskets

Both of the willow wine cradles pictured were made by the same method and using the same material as the hampers and sewing baskets imported by the Shakers for sale in their stores. The style and design of each is a bit different from the other. One has a handle over the top, while the other has a handle on the back. The plainer one is stamped "Indo-China (the name of a store that is not legible) and housewares, Boston."

Older wine cradle with handle over the top. 9½" l, 4" w, 7½" h. $25–$45

Wine cradle made in Indochina. 13" l, 4" w, 5½" h. $17–$30

It appears that a wide range of items were made in this style and using the same material. More research is definitely called for. All of these items were bought in antique shops.

Winnebago Indians

Along about 1000 A.D., the Winnebagos began migrating from the upper Mississippi Valley to the Green Bay area of Wisconsin. Overall, the move took centuries.

The Winnebago Indians were a more or less nomadic group consisting of fine hunters and fishermen. Because they lived so far north it was difficult for them to become very dependent on agriculture—the growing season was too short. They might have planted a little bit of corn, and maybe some squash, but they depended mainly on fishing and hunting.

Elm-splint basket. 8" dia, 10" o.h. $25–$40

They had access to many basketry materials and utilized most of them, especially birch bark, elm splints, and sweet-grass, which they usually sewed on with black thread. They also used ash splints and willow.

Winnowing Basket

The white settlers used a winnowing basket for separating chaff from grain and dirt from seeds, and also for a few other chores. The western Indians used it for dirt, chaff, and leaves from edible nuts picked up in the forest. In the South it was used for winnowing corn, rice, and other foods. The old winnowing baskets made by some of the western tribes are more interesting because they were used both for winnowing and cooking. This eliminated some work, as hot coals were placed in the basket after the nuts were gathered. In some instances, the tray was agitated as the nuts cooked, so the nuts winnowed and cooked at the same time. Roasted or parched nuts could be preserved longer than fresh ones.

Cane-winnowing or corn-sifting baskets. $100–$150

Wire Baskets

Not all old baskets were woven, coiled, or twined out of native materials—some were factory-made of wire. Since the factory-made wire baskets are becoming more common at antique shows, shops, and malls, they are included here. In antique places, these baskets are called by various names, such as potato, egg, or apple baskets. They were used in some of the old general stores to display fruit, eggs, and potatoes.

Large basket, 14" dia, 10½" h, $15–$23; small basket, 6¼" dia, 4¼" h, $5–$9

Wire Grass

Wire grass is one of a variety of grasses that grows over much of the United States, and at one time grew so abundantly in southeast Alabama that the county seat of Houston became known as "the Hub of the Wiregrass," a name it retains to this day. Around 1900, the newspaper in Dothan, Alabama (the county seat) was called *The Wiregrass Siftings.*

Wiregrass is a tall plant that grows to heights of 3 to 4 feet. It grows wild in the lowlands, especially the sandy lowlands of the South. It also grows in certain marshy areas. Although little information could be found on the use of wiregrass in the Deep South, it is known to have been quite popular during the turn-of-the-century basketry revival when it could be bought in the same stores that sold reed and rattan.

Wisteria Vine

Wisteria is a woody-looking vine of the pea family named for Caspar Wistar (1761–1818), an American anatomist. It grows best in the southern and eastern states. Most of the flowers are purple or white and look like large bunches of grapes. In the South, the plant is cultivated, but when new growth starts on the trees, it can cover them in a short amount of time. The wisteria vine is a fast-growing plant, which makes it a natural for basketmakers. The vines can be used in either their natural state or peeled. Peeling is easy if a knife is run down one side of the vine. When the bark is left on, its

Wisteria vine and Hong Kong grass basket. 10" dia, 5" h. $20–$29

grayish-green color gives the basket an instant antique appearance. Wisteria was often mixed with grape and honeysuckle vines to make baskets.

Wooden Bead Baskets

Around 1920 to 1925, the use of wooden beads in basketry became popular. The beads were made in a variety of sizes and in many types of wood. Seldom were the beads left natural; instead, they were painted all the colors of the rainbow. They were machine-made, which meant they were cheaper than handmade ones.

Circa 1925 basket with handle originating from the wooden base and decorated with orange beads. 8" dia, 14" o.h. $15–$25

By this time baskets weren't needed as much as they had been earlier, so the ladies made fancier baskets. They not only made baskets using wooden beads, but they also made all sorts of exciting things like trays, boudoir lamps, and floor lamps.

Wooden-Bottomed Baskets

Many baskets will be found with wooden bottoms. Some are new ones, coming in from as far away as Bangladesh, but a large number of older baskets have wooden bottoms, including the Nantucket Lightship baskets. When basketry experienced its revival in the 1950s, many beginners preferred making baskets, serving trays, and other basketry items on a wooden base. This was easier, as holes were bored into the plywood and the spokes fastened easily. This way, the spokes and weavers became one and the same. See "Fifties Baskets."

Work Baskets and Workbaskets

The term *work basket* is applied to two entirely different types of baskets. One is the work, burden, or farm basket—the type farmers would use in their work. The other type is a *sewing basket,* usually an open one, which is called a *workbasket* (one word, not two) in some parts of the country where the terms are interchangeable.

Beautifully woven, old oak-splint half-bushel farm or work basket. $75–$125

Large swing-handle farm basket. 18" dia, 13" h. $300–$400

Ash-splint swing-handle basket, damaged. $250–$300

Workbasket, Open

This is a workbasket of the sewing variety. Workbaskets were more popular during the earlier years, but some were made well into the tourist-trade years. Some are plain, so they can be used for other purposes, while many have small baskets or pockets inside so they be used as fitted sewing baskets. Without the pockets, they make excellent scrap baskets, or baskets to hold knitting and crochet threads.

Open work basket of ash splint. 9½" dia, 5" o.h. $35–60

Basket made of finely split oak splints. 9" dia, 9" o.h. $250–$450

Square ash-splint workbasket. Wide band near the top outlined with narrow black splints. 11" sq, 4¼" h. $55–$79

Woven Baskets

Actually, there are only two basic methods of basketry: weaving and coiling. The mystery, intrigue, and beauty of baskets comes from the many different way of weaving and coiling. Twining is an example: It is basically weaving but with a flair, such as twisting two very small, flexible weavers together between each spoke. Different types of weaves may be used.

Covered basket woven of wide and narrow ash splints. 13" dia, 11" h. $75–$115

Woven and Coiled Basket, New

It isn't often that more than one type of construction is used in a single basket. Several different materials may be used, but the maker usually stays with a single type construction.

In this basket, probably made in Hong King, at least two types of construction are used—hexagon weave and coiling. The cover is fastened onto the handle with basketry rings that allow it to be pushed up or down but not taken off.

Although this basket isn't very old, this type is being collected. Good old baskets are so hard to find and so expensive today

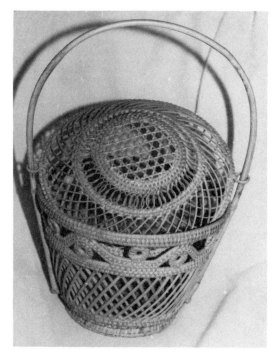

New Oriental basket. 9½" dia, 9½" h, 16½" o.h. $16–$25

that baskets like this are being seen more and more often in antique shops and shows.

X-Binding

An *X-binding* on a basket is the same as a double-wrapped rim, but this name is used more often because it's more descriptive. See "Double-Wrapped Rim."

Yahi Indians

The Yahi Indians of Southern California were and are a small and little-known band of the Yanas. When the white settlers arrived the Yahi were a handsome and fit tribe who believed in war, after the Indian fashion. They had great faith in themselves and felt they were superior.

Like all the other Indians they also made baskets using materials like hazel, redbud, willow, maidenhair fern, conifer, and bear grass. The one-rod coiling with spaced stitches was not the most popular style with them, but they are known to have made some pieces like this.

Covered storage basket. 17" dia, 20" h. $150–$200

Yarn Basket

A few years ago, no picture of a country home was complete without a basket full of yarn on the floor, or on a table near a comfortable rocker. That homey scene is still used today, but the baskets used in most of the pictures were made for another purpose (usually they were candy baskets).

Basketmakers of the Northeast made baskets specifically for yarn, because so many people in the area knitted. Ladies seldom went any place without bringing along their knitting; they continuously knitted warm clothing for the cold winters. Yarn baskets came in different sizes, in order to accommodate the needs of the knitter, no doubt. The handle could be slipped over the knitter's arm so she could take out the yarn without difficulty. The majority of the baskets were made of ash splints and sweet grass, but some can be found with the addition of Hong Kong grass.

Tall yarn basket of ash splints, sweet grass, and Hong Kong grass. 8" dia, 10" h, $45–$65; shorter basket, same materials, 8" dia, 6" h, $40–$55

Tall, square yarn basket made of ash splint and Hong Kong grass. 9" sq, 12" h. $40–$50

Yavapai Indians

Through the years there have been so many marriages between people of all tribes, as well as between Indians and whites, that it has become very difficult to attribute a bas-

Basket very similar to baskets made by the Yavapai. 13" dia. $500–$750

ket or type of basket to any one group unless the collector is very familiar with that type. This is especially true of the baskets of the Yavapai, who were closely associated with the Apache, as well as with other tribes in the area. Experts agree the Yavapai preferred to use less design than the Apache used. It is believed that they finished their baskets with a black border, although there are some exceptions. Devil's claw was used to make the black border.

Apparently, no new Yavapai baskets are being made, and a member of the tribal council says they are trying to locate authentic old baskets for display. The basket in the photograph is not an authenticated example, but it is very similar to the work done by the Yavapai.

Yellow Root

Both mountaineer and Cherokee basketmakers have long used the roots of a plant called *yellow root* to make yellow dye for the oak splints and cane used in their basketry.

Yew

Yew is an evergreen related to both pine and hemlock, which probably explains why it was used so much in basketry years ago.

The bark was used more than the wood, although the wood was close-grained and elastic when split into flexible flat weavers.

Yucca

Yucca is a plant of the lily family that grows abundantly in the arid Southwest. It has stiff, sword-shaped leaves that are used extensively by the Indians living in the area. They prefer the *plains* and the *banana* yucca. The leaves of the banana yucca are split and used as strips to make plaited or twilled baskets, while bundles of leaves may be used as a foundation for coiled baskets. The leaves are a delicate, natural shade, and the red roots can be used to make designs.

Plains yucca has a yellowish-green leaf that can be split and used the same as banana yucca. When cut narrow enough, the yucca strips resemble raffia and can be used the same way as raffia. Yucca leaves can be gathered any time of the year and used green, or they can be wrapped in a moist towel and kept in a damp place until needed. Yucca can be used much as the Afro-American or Gullah people of South Carolina use palmetto.

Yucca and devil's claw were used to make this beautifully designed tray. 15" dia. $425–$800

Zeh, Stephen

Stephen Zeh (pronounced *ZA*) is a contemporary Temple, Maine, basketmaker, who is striving to make baskets as well, or better than, other old-time New England basketmakers. He makes a beautiful brown-ash swing-handle in singles and in nesting sets of seven.

Nesting set of seven new baskets. 3" to 14" dia. $1995

Zhen (or Chen)

Through the years the *zhen,* or *chen,* most commonly associated with China and often called a pillow or head rest in America, has been made of three materials. First, they were made of porcelain with lovely designs; this type is quite rare now. Next, they were made of wood, and finally of bamboo. At different seasons of the year they were covered in different colors. Chances are the covers were beautifully embroidered silk.

Chinese bamboo zhen. 10" l, 4½" h. $25–$45

Zoar Community

In 1817, a group of approximately 400 people, who called themselves the Separatist Society of Zoar, migrated to America from Wurttemberg, Germany. They came to escape persecution for their religious beliefs, and found friends among the Quakers, who welcomed them and helped establish their settlement in Ohio. For the next 13 years, the community prospered and gained new members. Membership finally reached 500.

Little changed for them during the next 20 years—they continued farming and making baskets. When the leader, Baumeler, died in 1853, the community began to decline, and by 1898 its communistic features had been abolished. Like many other societies in America, the Zoar Community is known to have made and sold baskets of many types, but none has been found that could be authenticated.